The Layoff Playbook
What to Do Right Now

Copyright Disclaimer

Foreword

Take a deep breath in—and inhale the word new.
Exhale completely—with the word possibilities.

Let this be your mantra as you begin this book: New possibilities.

While a layoff can feel like the end of something solid, it's also the beginning of a new season.

I know this not just as a career coach, but as someone who has had to reinvent her own path more than once. I used to believe I had to plan every step, control every outcome, and force my way forward through overworking, pushing, and efforting. But it was only when things fell apart—when my carefully laid-out plans unraveled—that I discovered a better way.

It turns out, clarity doesn't come from pushing harder. It comes from slowing down, listening inward, and remembering why you're here.

You were born on this planet for a reason—not just to fill a role or meet expectations, but to be of service in a way that is deeply meaningful to you and profoundly needed by the world. You carry within you a unique life purpose that reveals itself over time. Sometimes, the most painful transitions are also the most powerful accelerators. A job loss may not have been your choice—but what happens next is.

Breathe in… new.
Breathe out… possibilities.

Take time to reflect. Let yourself feel. Let yourself dream again! Spend time in nature, in silence, and in inspiring places simply to hear your own voice again. Then begin this book. This is your chance to co-create with the universe. Step into your next chapter not through sheer willpower—but through intrinsic curiosity.

What if anything were possible?
What kind of work would feel joyful, nourishing, alive?
What impact do you want to make?
What causes matter to you?

These questions are not easy. But the right questions rarely are. Your responses are your cues. Start there.

Step by step, you'll find yourself on a new path—one that's more aligned, more impactful, and more you than anything you could have scripted. This is what I believe happens when life throws you a curveball at work. You're not being cast out. You're being called deeper in. You're being invited to remember your purpose—not as a job title, but as a way of living. And while that may sound poetic, I know you also need something practical. That's why this book matters.

Dr. Binta Brown has written the clearest, kindest, most grounded guide I've seen for navigating the messy, vulnerable reality of a layoff. She speaks from the heart and from experience. She offers structure and strategy without ever losing compassion. She doesn't bypass the hard parts or sugarcoat the truth, and she won't let you forget who you really are.

So if you're holding this book with shaky hands and a heavy heart—breathe.
You are not broken... You are becoming.
You are not failing... You are being redirected.
May this be the beginning of something more authentic and fulfilling than you ever could have imagined.

And may this mantra carry you through:
New possibilities.

– Lynn Chang, PhD, RYT, Founder of Career Zen

My Commitment To You

A layoff can feel like a gut punch—unexpected, disorienting, and deeply personal. You may not have chosen this moment, but you *do* get to choose how you respond.

This isn't a book about staying stuck.
It's not about waiting for the next job to land.

This is a results-driven guide to help you take control of your choices, your story, and your next chapter.

Inside, you'll find practical tools, proven strategies, and clear action steps to help you navigate each phase of transition with clarity and confidence—from stabilizing your finances and understanding your legal rights to refining your career brand and activating your network.

Let's get to work.
Your comeback starts now.

Table of Contents

You're Not Alone—And You're Not Powerless

I know this because I've been there.

My own layoff was public. My name, salary, and contributions were listed online for all to see. It was painful. Disorienting. And it felt deeply unfair. But that moment forced me to reimagine my career, take control of my future, and build something more aligned. This playbook isn't just built on theory, but grounded in lived experience. And if I could navigate through it, so can you.

Losing a job is a financial and emotional disruption. Whether this layoff took you by surprise or confirmed a quiet knowing, you might be feeling frustration, grief, self-doubt, or even relief laced with uncertainty. All of these are normal. All of them are valid.

You'll meet others in these pages—people who turned layoffs into pivots, launched businesses, or simply reclaimed clarity and confidence. Their stories are here to remind you: this chapter is hard, but it's also full of possibility.

Here's what's true:
A layoff does not define you.
It does not erase your skills, your impact, or your future.

Many professionals emerge from this moment stronger, clearer, and more aligned than before.

The Layoff Playbook is your guide for doing just that, on your terms. Whether your next move is a new job, freelance work, a career pause, or a full reinvention, this resource will walk with you step by step. You don't need to figure everything out today. You just need to take the next right step.

Let's do that, together.

🖊 Need space to process and reflect?
Pair this playbook with **The Layoff Comeback Journal,** a space to track your growth, gather insight, and build momentum as you move forward.
📖 Available on Amazon. Scan the QR code to learn more.

HOW TO USE THIS PLAYBOOK

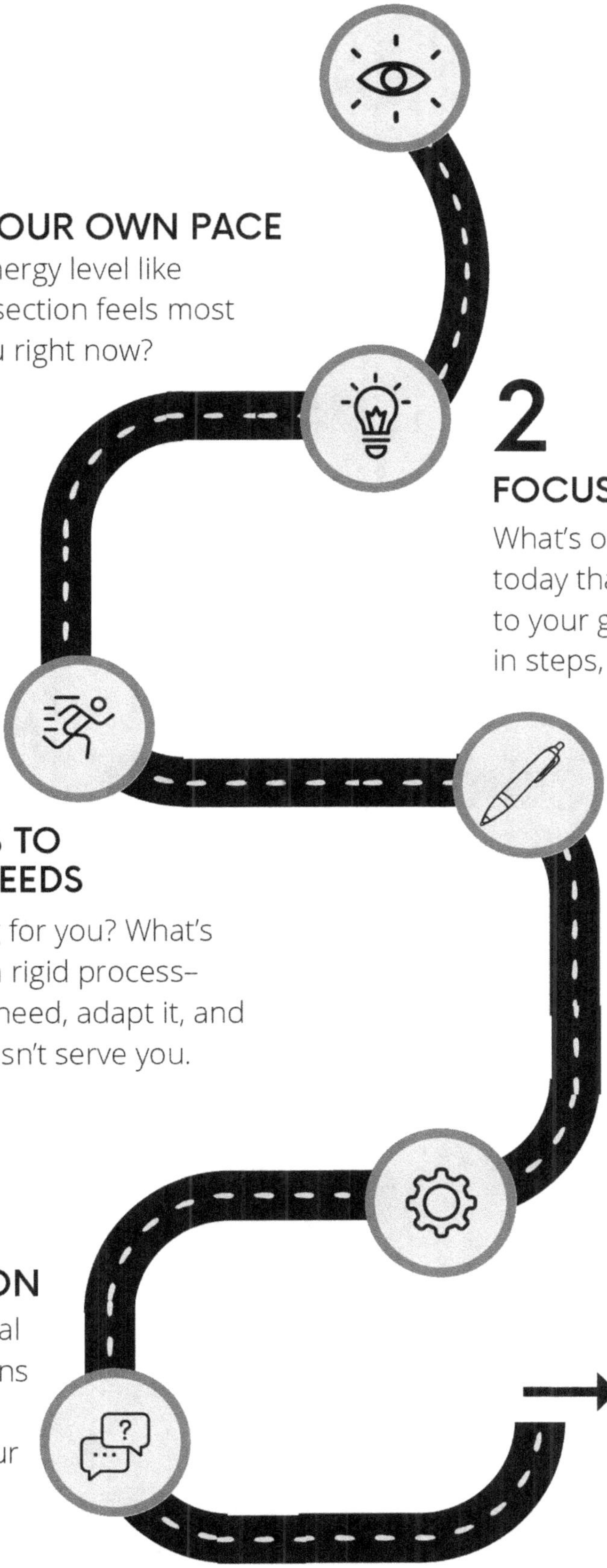

1
WORK AT YOUR OWN PACE
What's your energy level like today? Which section feels most relevant to you right now?

2
FOCUS ON SMALL WINS
What's one thing you can do today that will bring you closer to your goal? Progress happens in steps, not leaps.

3
ADJUST STRATEGIES TO FIT YOUR NEEDS
What's working for you? What's not? This isn't a rigid process– take what you need, adapt it, and leave what doesn't serve you.

4
SHARE AND DISCUSS
Discuss your playbook progress with others for valuable external perspective.

5
TAKE ACTION
Remember, real change happens when you implement your plans.

→ **POSSIBILITIES**

In the Aftermath
Legal & Strategic Matters

Before you dive into recovery plans or job search strategies, it's critical to pause and get informed. This section equips you with essentials many people overlook: understanding your rights under laws like the WARN Act, spotting red flags before layoffs happen, securing key documents, and using AI as a career accelerator. Whether your layoff just occurred or you're navigating uncertainty, these insights will help you protect what matters and move forward on solid ground.

Legal Considerations
Post-Layoff

Reviewing your severance agreement carefully can protect your future career flexibility and reputation. Pay close attention to terms like *non-compete*, *confidentiality*, and *non-disparagement agreement*, as these can significantly impact your next steps. If you're uncertain about any details, consider seeking guidance from a labor attorney or accessible online legal services.

Understanding Your Rights: The WARN Act
The Worker Adjustment and Retraining Notification (WARN) Act is a federal law that requires employers to provide advance notice of qualifying plant closings and mass layoffs. Knowing your rights under WARN can help you manage the uncertainty and disruption following a layoff.

When Does WARN Apply?
Your employer is typically required to comply if:
- They have 100+ full-time employees AND
- They plan to lay off employees at a single worksite in one of these ways:
  - Laying off 500 or more employees at the single worksite OR
  - Laying off 50-499 employees at the single worksite IF these employees make up at least 33% of the active workforce at that site.

Quick Steps to Confirm WARN Compliance
1. Review Communication: Check emails, letters, or notices you've received. WARN notices must be written and specific about layoff details (e.g., date, number of employees affected).

2. Clarify with HR: Contact your company's HR or Employee Relations department to confirm WARN notification details.

3. Verify with Trusted Legal Resources: If you suspect non-compliance, use official legal websites to understand your rights:
- National Conference of State Legislatures (NCSL) – Provides state-specific labor laws and updates.

- U.S. Department of Labor (DOL) – Outlines WARN Act requirements and worker protections.
- Legal Aid at Work – A nonprofit offering free legal information and support for employees.

Where to Learn More
For the most current and detailed information about the WARN Act and state-specific requirements, visit:
- U.S. Department of Labor WARN Act page. Scan the QR code to access it.

- Your state's labor department website for state-specific mini-WARN Acts. You can find the website by searching for "**[State Name]** Department of Labor" or "**[State Name]** Workforce Commission".

Possible Signs of an Impending Layoff (if WARN doesn't apply):
If your company isn't legally required to issue WARN notices, pay attention to these common indicators:
- Sudden hiring freezes or withdrawal of job postings.
- Significant budget cuts, reduction in spending, or canceled projects.
- Key executives leaving or restructuring.
- Delayed promotions, unusual budget-tightening measures, or unusual activity from leadership.
- Abrupt, increased confidentiality around financial reports and internal communications.

Being proactive and informed about your rights and available resources can significantly enhance your ability to effectively manage the stress and practical implications resulting from a layoff.

Legal Aid & Layoff Rights: Essential Resources

If you're uncertain about your rights during severance negotiations or suspect wrongful termination, consider reaching out to these reputable resources:

- **National Employment Lawyers Association (NELA)**

Website: www.nela.org

Assistance with finding attorneys specializing in employment law.

 Scan the QR code to access this site.

- **Local Legal Aid Societies**

Search online with prompts like: "Free legal aid for employment issues in **[Your City/State]**."

Protect What Matters:
Securing Your Career Essentials

It's easy to overlook your career essentials—until you need them. Whether a layoff is sudden or something you sense is coming, a few proactive steps can help you stay ready and reduce unnecessary stress. From saving key documents to gathering personal contacts, this chapter helps you prepare with intention so you can respond strategically, not reactively.

Collect Personal Contact Information
Save the personal (non-work) emails and phone numbers of trusted colleagues, mentors, and supervisors. If systems are deactivated suddenly, these connections can be crucial for referrals, networking, and future collaborations.

Archive Your Wins & Work Samples
Save examples of your strongest work—presentations, reports, campaigns, product designs, or strategy decks—alongside performance reviews, kudos emails, and client testimonials. These materials are essential for resumes, portfolios, interviews, and even severance negotiations. Store them on a personal device or cloud folder outside company systems to ensure access when needed.

Secure Copies of Important HR Documents
Save your offer letter, employment contract, benefits summary, and recent performance appraisals. Don't forget to download or screenshot your most current official job description. It can help you verify responsibilities, tailor future applications, and advocate for your value during transitions. These documents may become inaccessible post-layoff, so store them safely in a personal drive or folder.

Update Professional References
Reach out in advance to former managers, peers, or collaborators to confirm they're open to serving as positive references. A quick check-in now avoids last-minute scrambles and builds stronger endorsements.

Prepare For System Lockouts

Record important details like employee ID numbers, payroll or intranet logins, and benefits contacts in a secure personal file. If access disappears overnight, you'll still have what you need to file for unemployment, COBRA, or continue medical coverage.

Smarter, Not Harder: Using AI to Accelerate Your Job Search

Artificial Intelligence (AI) is transforming how we work, learn, and navigate career transitions. Whether you're refining your resume, prepping for interviews, or researching new roles, AI can amplify your efforts if you know how to use it well.

But here's the catch: many job seekers either don't use AI at all or rely on it too heavily without applying critical judgment. This chapter—and the prompts throughout this playbook—will help you use AI as a strategic co-pilot: one that saves you time, unlocks new insights, and strengthens your career story without losing your voice.

Why You Need to Learn AI Now

☑ **It's a Core Career Skill:** AI is reshaping nearly every industry. Whether or not you work in tech, knowing how to leverage AI tools can give you a serious edge, both as a job seeker and a professional.

☑ **It Boosts Efficiency:** AI can help draft resumes, tailor applications, rewrite LinkedIn summaries, or prepare interview responses, so you can spend more time networking and exploring meaningful roles.

☑ **It Enhances Strategic Thinking:** Use AI to uncover hiring trends, brainstorm transferable skills, or refine your positioning. AI won't replace human intuition, but it's a powerful brainstorming and research tool when used thoughtfully.

Ethical Use of AI: Important Considerations

While AI can be a game-changer, it's important to use it ethically critically, and responsibly.

🌟 **AI is a Tool, Not a Substitute for Judgment:** Always review, customize, and fact-check AI-generated content. Employers value your unique voice and real experiences. Use AI to support—not replace—your insight.

🌟 **Accuracy Isn't Guaranteed:** AI can misinterpret context, present outdated information, or even fabricate details. Verify any advice it gives, especially for job applications, salary research, or interview prep.

🌟 **Protect Privacy & Confidentiality:** Avoid sharing sensitive personal details, proprietary company information, or confidential job search data when using AI tools. Stick to generalized descriptions and remove identifiable information before inputting into AI.

🌟 **Use AI to Support, Not Mislead:** AI should enhance your career efforts, not inflate your qualifications or fabricate achievements. Avoid using it to generate false or misleading application materials.

🌟 **Transparency and Disclosure:** If you use AI to support your materials (e.g., generating resume bullet drafts or LinkedIn summaries), you don't necessarily need to disclose it. However, if you're in a creative or technical role (like writing, design, or data science), be prepared to speak to how you used AI and what decisions you made yourself.

🌟 **Be Mindful of Inclusive Practices:** AI tools may inadvertently reflect biases present in their training data. When using AI for tasks like interview preparation or career advice, ensure the content aligns with inclusive practices and does not perpetuate stereotypes.

🌟 **Staying Current in AI Policies in Hiring:** Some companies are now using AI-powered screening tools (e.g., resume scanners, video interview analyzers). Being aware of this trend helps you tailor materials accordingly while knowing your rights. Keep up with evolving regulations (e.g., the EEOC's stance on algorithmic bias) and know when you can ask about how your application is being assessed.

PHASE 1
Immediate Steps to Recovery

THE POWER OF THE PAUSE

You don't have to do everything at once. In fact, you shouldn't.

The day I was laid off, I didn't update my resume. I didn't rush to polish my LinkedIn. I didn't send a single application. Instead, I went outside. I grabbed my shears and my gloves, and I started working in the garden. I cleared out what was no longer thriving. I pulled the dead weight. I turned over the soil. And as I worked, I realized I wasn't just preparing the ground for new growth, I was preparing myself.

That quiet, messy, necessary work of tending to the soil mirrored exactly what I needed inside. To reset. To release. To make space for what might come next, even if I couldn't see it yet. I want you to know you don't have to figure everything out right now. You don't have to "fix" your career today. You don't have to leap into action before you've had a chance to breathe.

Instead, find your garden, whatever that is for you. Go for a walk. Sit in stillness. Take a nap. Cry. Pray. Rest. Layoffs are not just logistical events; they are emotional ruptures. They shake the ground beneath us.

And before you start building what's next, you deserve a moment to touch the earth again, literally or figuratively. **Truly, don't skip it!**

Growth takes time. There is work ahead. But first, ground yourself. Clear the space. Prepare the soil. Because what's coming next needs room to root. And so do you.

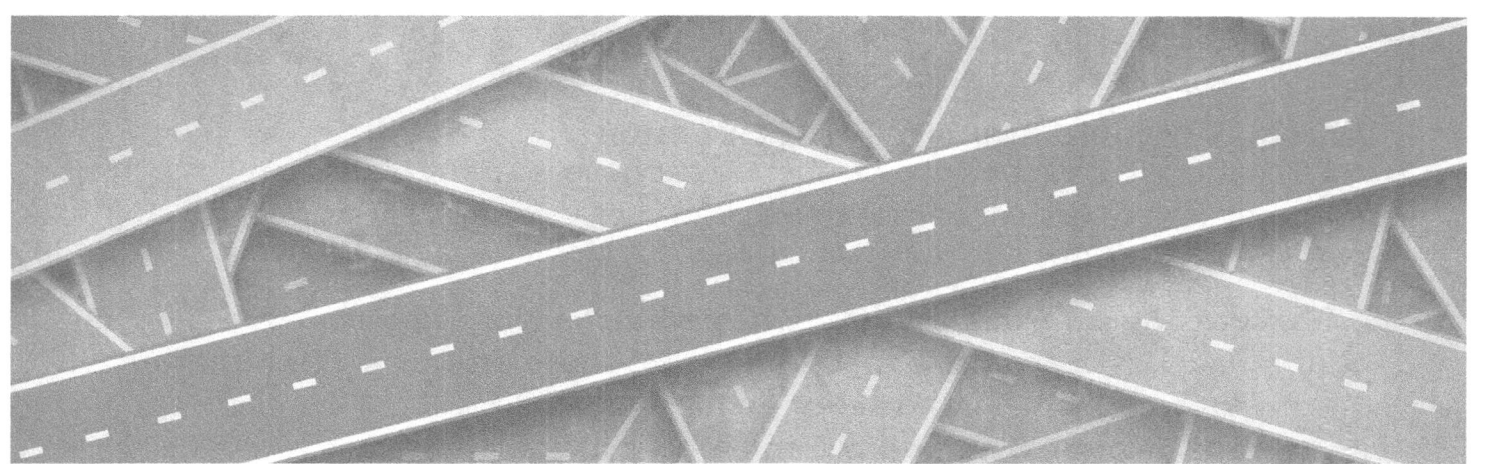

Your Layoff Recovery Roadmap: The First 90 Days

A strategic layoff recovery plan is about taking thoughtful, purposeful steps that restore your energy, protect your well-being, and position you for what's next.

Before diving in, remember:
- You don't have to do everything at once.
- Progress is not always linear.
- Small, consistent steps rebuild momentum.

Weeks 1-2: Stabilize & Regroup

The first two weeks are about emotional recovery, financial grounding, and gathering your career essentials. You don't need to take massive action—just focus on steadying your footing.

☑ **Acknowledge the Impact:** Allow space to process the layoff. It's normal to feel a mix of shock, grief, anger, or even relief. Permit yourself to feel without rushing to fix.

☑ **File for Unemployment Immediately:** Apply as soon as possible through your state's portal. Benefits can take time to process, and early filing helps avoid delays. (Scan the QR code on page 55.)

☑ **Review Health Insurance Options:** Assess COBRA, ACA marketplace plans, or spousal benefits to maintain coverage. Use this time to ask questions and understand your costs.

☑ **Assess Financial Needs**: Identify essential expenses and make adjustments. Use a simple monthly snapshot to reduce spending while you regroup.

☑ **Apply for Assistance or Relief Programs:** Research local hardship funds, rental assistance, and utility support if needed.

Weeks 3-6: Build Stability & Set Direction

Now that the initial shock has settled, this phase is about building momentum—financially, emotionally, and professionally. Focus on actions that move you from reaction to response.

☑ **Explore Short-Term Income:** Look into freelance work, consulting, staffing agency contracts, or part-time roles. These provide income without long-term commitment and keep your skills sharp.

☑ **Refresh Resume & LinkedIn:** Begin updating your materials with a focus on clarity and alignment. Highlight recent impact, relevant keywords, and a headline that reflects your direction, not just your past. (See page 126.)

☑ **Clarify Your Career Direction:** Use tools like CareerOneStop to explore emerging roles, identify transferable skills, and pinpoint training options. Their Local Help tool can connect you to job centers and reskilling programs nearby.

Use CareerOneStop to explore new career paths, identify transferable skills, and access tools to help define your next move. It offers free resources for training, job search, local support services, and more. **Bonus:** Use their Local Help tool to find support services in your area.

☑ **Reconnect With Your Network:** Don't just ask for a job, share your story, update your contacts on your goals, and ask for advice or insights. Rebuilding relationships now sets the stage for warm leads later.

☑ **Start Interview Prep Gently:** Use the ROAR framework to draft 1–2 stories that highlight your achievements, especially those showing adaptability. Practice responding to common questions, especially around your layoff, with clarity and calm. (See pages 71, 144, and 159.)

Weeks 7-12: Strategy, Positioning & Growth

This is the season of refinement. You've stabilized. You've started reconnecting. Now it's time to sharpen your strategy, align your message, and pursue opportunities with more clarity and momentum.

☑️ **Refine Your Target Roles & Positioning:** By now, you've gained insight from reflection, feedback, and research. Refine the kinds of roles, organizations, and environments you're aiming for, and update your materials and pitch to match.

☑️ **Tailor Your Applications Thoughtfully:** Instead of applying broadly, focus on customizing applications for 1–3 well-matched roles per week. Target quality over quantity and align your messaging to each company's needs.

☑️ **Deepen Interview Practice:** Build confidence through repetition. Use AI tools or peers to simulate interviews. Refine your responses using the ROAR method and rehearse your salary conversation scripts. (See page 144.)

☑️ **Negotiate Smartly:** If you're nearing an offer, review total compensation (not just salary). Consider benefits, flexibility, growth potential, and values alignment. Prepare a value-based negotiation strategy using scripts on pages 165, 168-169.

☑️ **Stay Flexible With Opportunities:** Consider fractional or project-based roles aligned with your skill set. They can lead to longer-term options or even full-time offers.

☑️ **Keep Learning:** Don't wait to be hired to grow. Continue upskilling with short courses or self-directed projects that demonstrate initiative and enhance your value in the market.

Fastest Ways to Earn Income After a Layoff: 5-Day Action Plan (Flex Plan)

This flexible 5-day plan is designed to help you take immediate, informed action toward earning income after a layoff, while recognizing that your situation is uniquely yours.

Whether you're ready to reenter full-time work, need to bridge a financial gap quickly, or want to experiment with entrepreneurial paths, this plan guides you through clear steps to regain financial stability without burning out.

Choose Your Income Path

Path	Best If...	Considerations	Steps
Full-Time Job	You want stability and your industry is hiring	May take time; depends on demand and network strength	Refresh your resume and start targeted outreach
Bridge Job	You need income fast and are open to temporary work	Helps reduce financial stress but may be less fulfilling	Explore local hiring boards or staffing agencies
Gig Work/ Entrepre- neurship	You want flexibility and have skills to monetize	Can take longer to stabilize income	List 3 monetizable skills or services to test
Portfolio Approach	You want a mix of stability and flexibility	Requires balancing multiple commitments	Map 2–3 income streams with the potential work hours per week
Fractional	You have deep expertise and seek high-value, short-term roles	Ideal for senior-level professionals; income can be significant but less predictable	Identify 2 firms or platforms hiring fractional talent

Key Questions to Reflect On
Before choosing your path, pause and ask:

- How urgently do I need income?
- How strong and active is my professional network?
- Are there immediate opportunities in my current industry right?
- Am I emotionally, mentally, and logistically ready to pursue full-time work immediately?
- Am I open to temporary roles, freelance work, or side gigs during my search?
- Could combining multiple income streams provide the stability I need right now?

Guided Reflection: What's My Best Next Step

There's no single "right" decision after a layoff—only the best next move for your current reality. Use this short reflection to clarify where to begin:

"Based on my current financial needs, energy levels, network strength, and career goals, the best next step for me right now is to explore _____. I'm open to reevaluating in 2–4 weeks as I learn more."

PRO TIP: Start With Now. If you're unsure which path to pursue, begin with what meets your most immediate needs. You can always pivot. The goal is to create short-term security while staying connected to long-term vision.

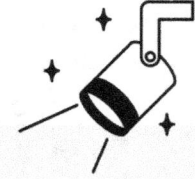

Building Stability One Stream at a Time

When **Rachel**, a New York-based graphic designer, was laid off from her in-house role at a mid-sized tech company, she realized another full-time job wasn't her only option. To quickly stabilize her finances, she took a contract project with a local design agency and started freelancing, creating brand kits for small businesses. Within a month, she expanded her income further by running workshops for a nonprofit's youth design program. This variety of income sources didn't just pay the bills—it reignited her creative spark and expanded her network.

Takeaway: Stability can come from multiple streams rather than a single job. Temporary or freelance work can serve as a meaningful bridge toward new possibilities, creativity, and growth.

From Pause to Progress: A 5-Day Reset Plan

The first few days after a layoff can feel disorienting. This 5-day plan offers structure without pressure, designed to help you reset emotionally, stabilize financially, and take small, meaningful steps forward.

Think of it as a reset, not a race. You just need a starting point that honors your energy and priorities.

Day	Focus	Goal
Day 1	Assess Finances	Understand your baseline needs and immediate options
Day 2	Identify Income Paths	Choose a direction based on your urgency and capacity
Day 3	Take Your First Steps	Initiate action—apply, reach out, or map your offer
Day 4	Expand Your Reach	Boost visibility through networking and connection
Day 5	Reflect & Adjust	Evaluate what's working and refine your strategy

Day 1
Assess Your Immediate Income Needs

✅ **Calculate Essential Expenses**
- Identify non-negotiable costs like rent/mortgage, utilities, insurance, food, and transportation.
- How much do you need to cover 3, 6, and 12 months?

✅ **Check Your Financial Safety Nets**
- How long will your savings last?
- What unemployment benefits, severance, or health coverage options do you have?

✅ **Reflect on Your Capacity**
- How quickly do you need income to start flowing?
- What's your emotional and mental bandwidth for job searching, gig work, or launching something new?

Clear Step-by-Step Example: Calculating Your Financial Needs
Here's a practical step-by-step approach to calculating your immediate financial needs post-layoff:

1. List Monthly Expenses:
- Rent/Mortgage: $2,000
- Utilities (Electricity, water): $350
- Groceries: $500
- Dining Out: $200
- Debt Payment: $300
- Internet & Phone: $180
- Transportation (car payments, insurance, fuel): $700
- Healthcare premiums and medications: $250
- Childcare: $1,000
- Miscellaneous (essential subscriptions): $70
- Savings Contributions: $180

Total Monthly Essential Expenses: $5,730/month

2. Determine Current Savings and Available Cash:
- Checking account balance: $1,200
- Emergency savings: $3,000
- Total Available Funds: $4,200

3. Identify Immediate Financial Gap and Evaluate Next Steps:
- If your severance or unemployment income equals $0 initially:
- Total Monthly Income: $2,300/month
- Total Monthly Expenses: $5,730/month

Sample Monthly Budget After Layoff Income:

Source	Amount ($)	Notes & Adjustments
Unemployment Benefits	$1,800	Estimated monthly unemployment benefit
Gig/Freelance Work	$500	Temporary part-time freelance writing gigs
Total Monthly Income:	**$2,300**	

Monthly Expenses (Before and After Layoff Comparison):

Expense Category	Before Layoff ($)	After Layoff ($)	Adjustments & Trade-Offs
Rent/Mortgage	$2,000	$2,000 (no change)	Fixed housing cost, essential
Utilities	$350	$200 (negotiated reduced rate; conserving electricity/water)	
Groceries	$500	$350 (reduced through meal planning and bulk shopping)	
Dining Out/Entertainment	$200	$50 (significantly reduced dining out; limited to free entertainment)	
Debt Payments	$300	$100 (requested temporary payment reduction arrangements)	
Internet & Phone	$180	$120 (negotiated lower-cost internet and downgraded phone plan)	
Transportation (car, gas, insurance)	$700	$550 (carpooling, reducing non-essential driving, adjusting coverage to reflect lower mileage)	
Healthcare Premiums/Costs	$250	$250 (COBRA/ACA premium maintained)	
Childcare	$1,000	$500 (part-time childcare or shared babysitting arrangements)	
Miscellaneous (essential subscriptions)	$70	$20 (kept only essential subscriptions; canceled streaming services)	
Savings Contribution	$180	$0	
Total Monthly Expenses:	**$5,730**	**$4,140**	

Monthly Budget Summary:

Total Monthly Income (After Layoff): $2,300

Total Monthly Expenses (Before Layoff): $5,730

Total Monthly Expenses (After Layoff): $4,140

Surplus/Deficit: -$1,840 (Monthly Deficit)

Total Savings + Checking Balances: $4,200

- $4,200 would be sufficient to cover the budget deficit for 2 months.

Realistic Trade-offs Made:

- Negotiated expenses: Utilities rates renegotiated, adjusted childcare to part-time or shared care.
- Sacrificed discretionary spending: Reduced dining out, entertainment, and most subscriptions.
- Increased income through temporary freelance work: Leveraged immediate skill sets to bridge financial gaps.
- Financial behavior shift: Actively monitored spending with budgeting apps or AI-driven budget planners (Goodbudget, Ynab, Mcnarch).

PRO TIP: Making Tough Trade-offs Work for You

When faced with financial strain, not all trade-offs feel equal. Some sacrifices are inconvenient, while others can significantly impact your lifestyle and well-being. In my own experience, adjusting expenses strategically, rather than making extreme cuts helped me maintain stability without feeling deprived.

Financial Guidance Resources

Seeking reliable financial advice post-layoff? Here are trustworthy resources that offer clear, beginner-friendly assistance:

National Foundation for Credit Counseling

Website: www.nfcc.org

Offers free or low-cost counseling to help you manage debt, budgets, and financial planning.

Benefits.gov

Helps you check eligibility for over 1,000 benefit programs. Includes a questionnaire that guides you to resources based on your needs.

Local Community Financial Literacy Programs

Find beginner-friendly local financial workshops by searching "**[Your City]** financial literacy workshops."

ACTION STEP: Complete the financial needs calculation using the sample budget template on page 37 to clarify your runway.

Sample Budget

Category	Planned Amount	Actual Amount	Difference	Notes (Cost-Cutting Ideas)
Income				
Primary Income				
Other Income (Side Gigs, Unemployment, etc.)				
Essential Expenses				
Housing (Rent/Mortgage)				
Utilities (Electricity, Water, Internet)				
Groceries				
Insurance (Health, Car, Home)				
Transportation (Gas, Public Transit)				
Debt Payments (Loans, Credit Cards)				
Healthcare/Medication				
Child Care				
Non-Essential Expenses				
Dining Out/Takeout				More home cooked meals
Subscriptions (Streaming, Apps)				Cancel unused ones
Shopping (Clothing, Extras)				Consider thrift and consignment stores
Entertainment (Movies, Events)				Find free community activities
Savings & Emergency Fund Expenses				
Emergency Fund Contribution				
Retirement Savings				
Total Expenses				
Remaining Balance				

Choose the Best Path for Now

Once you have clarity on your financial picture, the next step is deciding what kind of income strategy makes the most sense for you right now. This decision will guide how you approach the next steps in this plan.

Ask yourself:
- How urgently do I need to replace my income?
- Do I want stability, flexibility, or just a temporary solution?
- What's realistic for me, given my industry and current job market conditions?

Here are five paths you can choose from:

Option 1: Pursue a Full-Time Job

If your priority is securing another full-time role in your field or an adjacent industry, focus your efforts on applying to open roles and networking intentionally.

✅ Best if you prefer long-term stability, benefits, and a steady paycheck. Especially effective if your skills are in demand and your industry is hiring.

Option 2: Secure a Bridge Job

This is temporary work that helps you stay financially afloat while you continue searching for your ideal role. Think contract work, part-time roles, seasonal positions, or remote customer service.

✅ Best if you need immediate income and want to ease financial stress without committing long term.

Option 3: Focus on Gig Work or Entrepreneurship

Leverage your skills through freelance work, side gigs, consulting, or creating digital products.

✅ Best if you want flexibility, already have marketable skills, or are curious about self-employment.

✅ May take longer to stabilize income, but offers creative control and potential future growth.

Option 4: Portfolio Approach

This is a blended path where two or more strategies (like a part-time bridge job plus gig work or freelance projects) are combined to diversify income while staying flexible.

✅ Best for those who want or are testing multiple income streams, or those who want security through multiple options.

This option is increasingly common in today's work landscape, especially for those with multiple skill sets or whose industries are in flux.

Option 5: Fractional/Interim Work

This path involves taking on high-level, part-time, or contract-based roles in which you contribute your expertise to organizations without a full-time commitment. You might serve as a part-time CMO, interim team lead, or fractional project consultant.

✅ Best for experienced professionals with specialized skills who want flexibility while still operating at a strategic level.

This option is growing rapidly in today's talent market, especially in startups, small businesses, or companies managing transitions. It allows you to stay engaged in meaningful work, command strong rates, and maintain control over your time.

Action Step:
Pick the path that best fits your needs and capacity right now.
☐ Full-Time Job
☐ Bridge Job
☐ Gig Work or Entrepreneurship
☐ Portfolio Approach (a mix of two or more strategies)
☐ Fractional

Reminder: There's no one right choice, and you can always pivot later. The goal today is to make a decision that supports your immediate financial well-being.

Need help narrowing it down?
Head back to the "Fastest Way to Earn Income After a Layoff" chapter on page 28 to revisit the five post-layoff income paths. Your notes or highlights from that section can help guide the path that makes the most sense for this week—no long-term commitment required.

Day 2
Identify Immediate Opportunities

Before you dive into action, check in: Does your chosen path still feel right? Adjust as needed.

Full-Time Job Focus:

✓ Update your resume and LinkedIn profile. Recruiters frequently search LinkedIn for candidates who match their open roles. Regularly refreshing your profile with recent experience, skills, and keywords from your desired positions makes your profile appear active and more likely to surface in recruiter searches.

✓ Set daily job application goals. Consistency builds momentum increases your chances of finding the right opportunity.

✓ Activate your network with a clear "I'm looking" message. Many job openings are filled through referrals before they're even posted.

Examples
- Reach out to past colleagues for referrals and warm introductions.
- Customize your resume using keywords and qualifications listed in the job descriptions you find most compelling.
- Apply to roles in your target companies.

Bridge Job Focus:

✓ Research local temp agencies, staffing firms, and part-time roles aligned with your transferable skills.

✓ Apply for local or remote quick-start roles (e.g., seasonal, customer support, admin, project-based work).

Examples
- Admin, project-based work, or customer service work.
- Remote administrative support.
- Food delivery or rideshare services.

Gig/Entrepreneurship Focus:
- ✅ Identify your top service or product idea.
- ✅ Create a simple offer (e.g., social media posts advertising your service).

Examples
- Selling digital products (templates, planners, guides) on Etsy, Gumroad, or Shopify.
- Offering freelance services (writing, design, admin support) on Upwork, Fiverr, or Freelancer.
- Launching coaching or consulting packages, such as:
  - Career Coaching: Helping job seekers prepare resumes, navigate job searches, or improve interview skills.
  - Social Media Consulting: Advising small businesses on creating effective social media strategies and campaigns.
  - Wellness Coaching: Guiding clients in setting health or fitness goals and developing personalized wellness plans.
  - Business Consulting: Supporting startups or entrepreneurs in streamlining operations, project management, or enhancing customer experience.

PRO TIP: Planning to sell digital products? Check out Etsy intro tutorials on YouTube to master keyword selection and competitive pricing. Explore Amazon best-sellers in your category and notice their presentation, descriptions, and marketing strategies. Understanding these patterns helps you position your product effectively and attract the right customers faster.

Portfolio Approach:
- ✅ Choose two complementary income streams to pursue in parallel.
- ✅ Balance time between stable income (bridge work) and scalable opportunities (gig work).

Examples
- Combine part-time work with freelance gigs.
- Do rideshare during the day and offer online workshops in the evening.

Fractional Work Focus:

✅ Identify your niche expertise and package it as a service (e.g., operations, marketing, HR, finance, tech).

✅ Research companies going through growth, transition, or leadership gaps —these are often the best fit for fractional support.

✅ Update your LinkedIn to reflect fractional availability and highlight the outcomes you deliver.

Examples
- Fractional Head of People for a scaling startup.
- Interim Operations Lead for a nonprofit during a leadership shift.
- Fractional Project Manager for a short-term digital transformation initiative.

PRO TIPS:
- Use LinkedIn and Google News alerts to identify companies experiencing funding rounds, leadership changes, or rapid growth. Search terms like "newly funded," "hiring surge," or "leadership transition" paired with your target industry. These signals often point to organizations in need of short-term strategic support, perfect for pitching fractional expertise.

- Utilize specialized platforms, leverage your network, and explore general job boards such as fractionaljobs.io, www.gofractional.com, and toptal.com. Some general job boards include flexjobs.com, globallyhired.com, and Indeed.com.

Day 3
Take Your First Step

Full-Time Job:
- ✓ Apply to 3–5 aligned roles.
- ✓ Send outreach messages to key contacts.

Examples
- Schedule informational interviews.
- Reconnect with professional groups.

PRO TIP: Informational interviews can be a game-changer in your job search. Aim to connect with professionals in roles or industries you're interested in to gain firsthand insights.

Prioritize contacting former colleagues, industry leaders, or professionals working at your target companies.

Use LinkedIn or alumni networks to find connections, and prepare thoughtful questions in advance to make the conversation meaningful.

Bridge Job:
- ✓ Submit applications to at least 3 quick-hire roles.
- ✓ Check for new opportunities on temp agency websites weekly.

Examples
- Apply for event-based roles.
- Check community boards for immediate openings.

Gig/Entrepreneurship:

 Announce your service or business offer publicly.

Pitch 3 potential clients.

Examples
- Post an offer on social media.
- Email past clients or contacts your business offer.
- Create a simple sales page.

Portfolio Approach:

Take your first action in both areas (e.g., apply to one bridge job and post your freelance offer).

Examples
- Balance part-time work with online sales.
- Split your day between freelance projects and job applications.

Fractional Work:

Identify 2–3 companies that could benefit from your expertise and reach out directly.

Draft and send a short message offering fractional support for a specific outcome.

Examples
- Pitch yourself as a temporary solution during a team transition.
- Re-engage former clients, employers, or collaborators with a value-driven update on your availability.

PRO TIP (for Fractional, Gig, or Portfolio paths):
Many decision-makers search LinkedIn and Google to find contractors, consultants, or fractional talent—often before posting a formal role. To increase your chances of being found:

- Use keywords in your LinkedIn headline that match the service or solution you provide (e.g., "Fractional HR Leader | Talent Strategy | Culture Consultant").
- Post a short LinkedIn update sharing what you do, who you help, and that you're open to fractional or project-based work.
- If you have a website or portfolio, include keywords related to the service you offer (like "resume writer," "fractional CMO," or "leadership coach") on key pages to show up in Google searches.

Remember: Visibility leads to opportunity, especially when people are quietly looking.

JOB SEEKER SPOTLIGHT

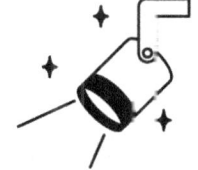

Clarity By Experimenting

After being laid off from his role managing student engagement programs at a regional Texas university, **Jordan** gave himself time to assess his finances and reflect on the kind of work that felt most energizing. Instead of rushing onto job boards, he reached out to a past nonprofit partner and offered short-term help designing their youth outreach curriculum. That small project helped him reconnect with his strengths and validate his value outside academia. Within three months, he had two more consulting clients and a clearer vision of the kind of impact he wanted to make moving forward.

Takeaway: Clarity doesn't always come before action. Small, aligned experiments can help you reconnect with your value and make decisions rooted in insight, not urgency.

Day 4
Expand Your Reach

Check in: Are you building momentum? Shift focus if another path feels more promising.

Full-Time Job:
Attend a virtual networking event or industry meetup.

Examples
- Join online industry groups.
- Participate in industry/skills-specific webinars.
- Share and comment on thought leadership posts.

Bridge Job:
✅ Contact two companies for short-term or part-time opportunities.
✅ Explore strategic volunteer roles that build community ties and industry exposure.

Examples
- Check local business forums and job boards for short-term gigs.
- Ask friends or former coworkers about temp openings.
- Visit nearby staffing agencies.
- Volunteer with local events or community orgs tied to your target industry (e.g., city events, arts organizations, local nonprofits).

PRO TIP: Volunteering is about giving back *and* it can be a strategic career move. Choose opportunities that align with your goals and give you a reason to show up, build connections, and be seen.

Gig/Entrepreneurship:
Reach out to your network for referrals.

Examples
- Ask for testimonials.
- Offer referral bonuses.
- Collaborate with complementary businesses.
- Participate in market research through sites like Respondent.io, UserInterviews, and UserTesting.

Portfolio Approach:
Leverage all parts of your professional identity. Cross-promote both paths.

Examples
- Advertise your freelance or consulting services within your full-time or former job network.
- Offer package deals that bundle your gigs (e.g., photography + editing, coaching + resume review).
- Post strategically on LinkedIn about what you're offering—share your expertise, client wins, or insights related to your services to attract aligned opportunities.

PRO TIP: Every post is a digital handshake. You never know who's watching, or who might refer you.

Here's a sample LinkedIn post template tailored for someone pursuing a Portfolio Approach—great for expanding reach while showcasing value, credibility, and professionalism:

LinkedIn Post Template
Header (Grab Attention):
Feeling grateful to support clients during this season of transition, and excited to offer even more value.
Body (Share What You're Doing + Who It's For):
In addition to [current or most recent role], I've been working with [audience or client type] on [type of work or service you offer].
Whether it's [example #1] or [example #2], I'm helping people [specific outcome you help them achieve].
If you (or someone you know) is looking for [quick benefit statement], I'd love to connect.
CTA (Call to Action):
- Feel free to message me directly or share this post with someone who might benefit.
- Let's build something meaningful—even in the in-between seasons.
Hashtags (Targeted):
#PortfolioCareer #CareerTransitions #ConsultingLife #FreelanceWork #JobSearchSupport

Fractional Work:
Position yourself as a strategic partner, not just a temporary fix. Expand your reach by showing up where decision-makers look for high-level support.

Examples:
- Post on LinkedIn with a clear offer: what you do, who you help, and the results you deliver in fractional roles.
- Reconnect with past employers, executives, or founders and share your availability for short-term or project-based support.

- Join communities or platforms where companies seek fractional talent (e.g., Bolster, Fractional Jobs, or niche Slack groups).
- Ask colleagues to tag or refer you when they hear of teams navigating transitions, growth, or leadership gaps.

PRO TIP: Visibility matters. Most fractional opportunities are filled through referrals, not job boards. Make it easy for people to connect the dots between their business needs and your expertise.

Day 5
Reflect and Adjust

For all paths:
- ✓ Assess what's working (and what's not.)
- ✓ Celebrate any wins, big or small.
- ✓ Decide if your current path still feels right, and make any necessary adjustments based on early results.

Final Check-In:

Based on your financial picture and current capacity:

☐ Are you ready to pursue a Full-Time job?

☐ Would a Bridge Job reduce financial stress?

☐ Do you want to explore Gig Work or Entrepreneurship?

☐ Or does a Portfolio Approach feel like the right mix?

ACTION STEP: Circle the option above that fits your current needs best. Then, take your first step with purpose—and give yourself credit for moving forward.

Mental Health Check-Ins: Managing Daily Anxiety

Navigating job loss can take a toll on your mental health. Daily check-ins can help maintain emotional balance.

Quick Daily Tips:
- **Start your day with a small ritual:** Brush your hair, wash your face, and get dressed—even if you're not going anywhere. This physical shift signals your brain that the day has started and you're in motion.
- **Get moving:** A short walk, stretching, or a quick workout—even 10 minutes—can help reset your mood, boost energy, and reduce anxiety.
- **Practice brief mindfulness (5–10 min):** Try deep breathing, grounding exercises, or simply sit quietly with your coffee before diving into your day.
- **Keep a "done" list:** Write down 1–3 small wins or completed tasks each day to stay motivated and acknowledge your progress.
- **Stabilize your rhythm:** Stick to consistent sleep, meals, and break times to support emotional regulation and productivity.

Digital Tools for Ongoing Support

Support your mental and emotional well-being with tools that fit your needs and lifestyle:
- **Calm (calm.com):** Mindfulness, guided meditation, sleep stories.
- **Headspace (headspace.com):** Quick meditations, stress management exercises.
- **BetterHelp (betterhelp.com):** Accessible online counseling services.

 AI Prompt: Create Mindfulness Routines

"Provide me with a simple daily mindfulness routine to help manage anxiety after my layoff."

✎ **Reflective Prompt:**
What did I learn about myself this week?
What surprised me, in a good way?
What's one thing I'm proud I did, even if it felt small?

Financial Stability After a Layoff: Planning & Resources

Navigating financial uncertainty after a layoff can feel destabilizing, but you're not powerless. Taking small, proactive steps to manage your benefits, protect your savings, and explore income opportunities can help you move from fear to financial clarity.

Maximizing Severance & Negotiation

☑ **Negotiate Extensions:** Ask about extending health benefits, payout timing, or additional compensation.

☑ **Request Outplacement Services:** Many employers offer career coaching or resume assistance—request these if available.

☑ **Lump Sum vs. Structured Payouts:** Consider how severance payments impact unemployment eligibility; lump sums provide flexibility, but structured payouts may extend financial stability.

PRO TIP: If your company offers a severance package, you may have more flexibility than you think. Instead of taking a lump sum payout for unused vacation time, consider negotiating to push out your end date using that accrued time.

This strategy can help you temporarily remain on payroll, extending access to company-provided health insurance and delaying the start of unemployment benefits if needed. Speak with HR to explore this option before signing any agreements.

⏰ **ACTION STEP:** If you've been offered severance, review the details carefully and negotiate extensions or benefits that could support your transition.

Applying for Unemployment Benefits: What to Expect
Unemployment benefits can provide financial relief, but they often do not replace your full salary. It's important to set realistic expectations.

☑ **How to Apply:** Visit your state's unemployment website and follow the application process. Be prepared to submit details about your previous employment and earnings.

☑ **Understanding Payouts:** Benefits vary by state. For example, currently in Texas, the maximum weekly benefit is $591, with a total maximum payout of $15,366 over 26 weeks.

 Scan the QR code for charts of weekly unemployment payments listed by state by the Center on Budget and Policy Priorities.

☑ **Work Search Requirements:** Most states require job search activities in order to continue receiving benefits. Keep track of applications and networking efforts.

☑ **Plan for a Financial Adjustment:** Since unemployment benefits may not fully cover your expenses, consider a budgeting strategy that combines benefits with short-term income options.

 **ACTION STEP:** Research your state's unemployment benefits and apply asap to prevent financial delays. Scan the QR code to access your state's unemployment office.

Securing Health Insurance

Losing employer-sponsored health insurance can be a major stressor. However, there are options to maintain coverage and ensure continuity of care.

✅ **COBRA Coverage:** If offered, COBRA allows you to continue your employer's health insurance for a limited time, though it may be expensive.

✅ **Marketplace Plans:** The Affordable Care Act (ACA) Marketplace offers alternative health insurance plans that may be more affordable than COBRA.

✅ **Medicaid or Spouse's Plan:** Depending on your income level, you may qualify for Medicaid, or you may be eligible to join a spouse's plan.

✅ **Prescription Planning:** Before your insurance expires, request a 90-day supply of necessary medications to avoid immediate coverage gaps.

ACTION STEP: Visit Healthcare.gov to explore affordable options.

Choosing the Right Healthcare Coverage: Practical Scenarios

To better illustrate how healthcare choices post-layoff impact your finances, consider these practical scenarios that illustrate realistic trade-offs and decisions individuals commonly face:

Scenario 1: COBRA vs. Affordable Care Act (ACA)

Family Type: John (Married, No Children)

Situation: John's COBRA option is $750/month; however, he finds an ACA marketplace plan for $450/month.

Decision: John selects the ACA plan, accepting slightly higher deductibles but significantly lower monthly premiums to extend his emergency savings while job hunting.

Scenario 2: COBRA vs. Spouse's Employer Plan

Family Type: Sophia (Married with Two Kids)

Situation: COBRA costs $1,200/month for her family. Her spouse's employer-sponsored family coverage option is $500/month.

Decision: They switch to the spouse's employer-sponsored plan, saving $700/month while maintaining adequate coverage.

Scenario 3: Medicaid as a Short-Term Solution

Family Type: Alex (Single Parent, Two Children)

Situation: Alex's monthly income is temporarily limited, qualifying him and his children for Medicaid coverage with no premium costs.

Decision: Alex enrolls temporarily in Medicaid, significantly reducing monthly healthcare costs while preserving financial resources to meet other essential expenses.

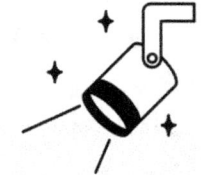

Stabilizing Quickly with Strategic Choices

After a sudden layoff from his role in the energy sector, **Felix,** a mid-career data analyst based in North Carolina, negotiated to extend his healthcare benefits by using unused PTO. He immediately applied for unemployment benefits and switched to a lower-cost ACA plan rather than paying higher COBRA premiums, helping stretch his savings further. To bridge the income gap while regrouping, Felix tapped into his professional network. A former colleague—now a close friend—connected him with a three-month contract role at their current company. This timely opportunity allowed Felix to avoid dipping into retirement funds, providing essential stability and giving him the breathing room to pursue his next full-time role with greater clarity and purpose.

Takeaway: Strategic use of available benefits and timely contract wins can transform a financial shock into a period of recovery, stability, and intentional growth.

Handling Retirement Accounts Wisely

Withdrawing funds from retirement savings may seem like a quick fix, but doing so often comes with long-term financial consequences. Understanding your options can help you make informed decisions.

☑ **Avoid Early Cash-Outs:** Withdrawing funds before age 59½ can result in a 10% early withdrawal penalty plus additional taxes.

☑ **Rolling Over to an IRA:** Instead of cashing out, consider rolling over your 401(k) into an IRA to maintain tax advantages and continued growth.

☑ **State Employee Pension Considerations:** If you have a pension through a state retirement system, cashing out may erase your years of service credit, impacting your ability to requalify for benefits if you return to government work.

☑ **Consult a Financial Advisor:** Each person's financial situation is unique. Speaking with a certified financial planner can help you evaluate the best course of action.

PRO TIP: Considering an IRA withdrawal after rolling over your 401(k)? Some situations, such as certain medical expenses, qualified education costs, or first-time home purchases, might qualify for penalty exceptions. Before making a move, check if your circumstances apply—and consult a financial advisor to explore your best options.

If You're Nearing Retirement

As you approach retirement, decisions about your 401(k), pension, or early withdrawals become even more critical. For example, some individuals consider rolling a traditional 401(k) into a Roth IRA during a lower-income year, but this can trigger tax consequences.

☑ Important: Consult a certified financial planner or tax professional before making retirement-related moves. The right guidance can help you navigate impacts on your long-term savings, Social Security timing, and Medicare eligibility.

You can find fee-only fiduciary advisors through sites like NAPFA.org or LetsMakeAPlan.org.

Should You Tap Your Retirement Savings? A Real-World Comparison

When laid off, tapping into your retirement savings may seem like a quick solution—but it's important to understand the true financial impact. Let's look at Angela's situation to explore the long-term cost of early withdrawal versus rolling over into an IRA.

👩 Angela's Retirement Savings Decision

- Age: 38 (below 59½, so early-withdrawal penalties apply)
- Retirement Account Balance: $10,000
- Withdrawal Amount: $10,000
- Federal Tax Rate: 22%

Option 1: Cashing Out (Early Withdrawal)

Description	Amount
Original Balance	$10,000
10% Early-Withdrawal Penalty	-$1,000
Federal Taxes (22%)	-$2,200
Net Amount Retained	**$6,800**
Total Immediate Loss	**$3,200**

Option 2: Rollover to an IRA

Description	Amount
Original Balance	$10,000
Early-Withdrawal Penalty	$0
Federal Taxes	$0 (if rolled over properly)
Amount Preserved	**$10,000**

Comparison & Implications:

Cashing Out:

- Immediate cash but with a significant reduction due to taxes and penalties.
- Less money available for long-term financial goals or retirement.

Rolling Over to an IRA:

- Preserves the full value of your savings.
- Avoids immediate tax impact.
- Keeps your future financial growth intact.

✍ **Reflection Prompt:**

If you're considering tapping into retirement savings, what's driving the urgency,and are there other options that could help without resulting in a long-term financial hit?

Try It Yourself: Plug in Your Own Numbers

Use this quick worksheet to estimate your own scenario. **Note:** This example assumes your entire retirement balance is being withdrawn. The calculation for a partial withdrawal would be different:

My Retirement Balance/Withdrawal Amount: _____
Age: ____ (Is penalty applicable?)
Estimated Tax Rate: ____%

Cashing Out:

10% Early-Withdrawal Penalty
      (Withdrawal Amount x 0.1): _____
Estimated Taxes
      (Total Withdrawal x Estimated Tax Rate): _____
Estimated Net Amount Retained
      (Retirement Balance - Penalty - Taxes): _____

Rolling Over to an IRA:

Estimated Amount Preserved
      (Full Amount Rolled Over): _____

Before making any decisions, consult a certified financial planner or retirement advisor for personalized guidance.

AI Prompt: Create a Personal Budget After Layoff

"Help me create a simple monthly budget based on an unemployment income of $_____, COBRA/ACA costs of $_____, and $_____ in savings. I want to identify essential expenses, areas to cut, and how long my savings might last."

ACTION STEP: Review your retirement plan options and schedule a consultation with a financial advisor before making any withdrawals.

A Balanced Approach
Cut Unnecessary Expenses *and* Expand Income:

Reducing spending is a good starting point, but it often leads to only modest savings. For example, cutting non-essential costs may save around $1,400 annually, which is helpful but not transformative. By also focusing time and attention on earning additional income, you can increase your financial security much faster. If you allocate time to leveraging skills, knowledge, or digital opportunities, you could potentially generate $20,000+ in additional income per year.

Expense Reduction Strategies

☑ **Pause/Eliminate Unnecessary Subscriptions:** Cancel streaming services, unused memberships, and premium accounts.

☑ **Negotiate Bills & Reduce Fixed Costs:** Contact service providers to lower interest rates, insurance premiums, and utility costs.

☑ **Use Cash-Back & Discount Programs:** Leverage apps like Rakuten, Honey, or cash-back credit cards to save on essential purchases.

PRO TIP: Trimming expenses is a great start, but pairing that with tools that stretch your budget can create real breathing room. Cashback apps like Rakuten partner with thousands of retailers to offer cashback on everyday purchases, while Honey automatically applies coupon codes at checkout to help you save instantly. These free tools make your regular spending work harder for you, so you can redirect more energy toward building your next income stream.

Income Expansion Strategies

☑ **Freelance or Consult:** Offer skills in writing, marketing, virtual assistance, coding, or coaching via platforms like Upwork or Fiverr.

☑ **Sell Digital Products:** Create templates, e-books, or online courses for passive income.

☑ **Offer a Service Locally:** Pet sitting, tutoring, delivery driving, or personal assistance gigs can generate quick income.

☑ **Leverage AI Tools for Side Work:** Use AI-powered content creation, transcription services, or virtual assistant platforms to help automate income generation.

ACTION STEP: Review your bank statements and identify one **cost-cutting** measure and one **income-generating** opportunity you can implement this week.

Final Thoughts

Financial recovery after a layoff is rarely linear, but it is entirely possible. With thoughtful decisions and small, strategic income moves, you create breathing room today and build security for tomorrow. Every informed step you take now is an act of protection and preparation.

Protect Your Peace
During Uncertainty

Losing a job can shake your confidence, but it does not define your skills, value, or future opportunities. Managing stress, maintaining self-confidence, and creating structure can help you regain control and move forward with resilience.

JOB SEEKER SPOTLIGHT

From Overwhelmed to Steady

After an unexpected layoff, **Tasha,** a Texas-based HR professional, found herself in a fog of exhaustion, uncertainty, and self-doubt. For two weeks, even the smallest tasks felt overwhelming. What helped her begin to shift? A simple daily routine and a peer accountability group that reminded her she wasn't alone. "Even brushing my teeth before 9 a.m. felt like a win," she shared. "That first week, I didn't need a job—I needed to feel human again."

Takeaway: Career recovery goes beyond income or interviews. It starts with emotional recovery, self-compassion, and restoring your sense of self.

Recognizing Burnout, Stress, & Emotional Impact

☑ **Acknowledge Your Feelings:** Shock, frustration, and anxiety are natural reactions. Allow yourself to process them.

☑ **Identify Signs of Burnout & Stress:** Difficulty concentrating, lack of motivation, and exhaustion may indicate emotional strain.

☑ **Reframe Negative Thoughts:** A layoff is a career transition, not a reflection of your worth.

ACTION STEP: Journal about your emotions and identify specific stressors impacting your well-being.

Creating a Structured Routine for Stability

☑ **Maintain a Daily Schedule:** Build structure into your day with job search activities, movement, and moments of rest.

☑ **Set Small, Achievable Goals:** Breaking tasks into manageable steps reduces overwhelm and helps you stay motivated.

☑ **Prioritize Wellness:** Activities like exercise, meditation, or hobbies support mental clarity and emotional resilience.

☑ **Engage with Others Through Service:** Volunteering your time or skills not only helps others—it reinforces your sense of purpose and keeps you connected during a time when isolation can creep in.

ACTION STEP: Design a daily routine to include structured job search time and self-care activities. Sample below. Adjust according to your needs/preferences.

Sample Schedule

Time	Activity
7:00 AM - 8:00 AM	Morning Routine & Self-Care (Meditation, Light Exercise, Healthy Breakfast)
8:00 AM - 9:00 AM	Daily Planning & Mindset Check-in (Journaling, Reviewing Goals)
9:00 AM - 10:30 AM	Job Search Focus (Resume Updates, LinkedIn Networking, Applications)
10:30 AM - 10:45 AM	Short Break (Stretch, Hydrate, Light Walk)
10:45 AM - 12:00 PM	Skill Building (Online Course, Industry Research, Mock Interviews)
12:00 PM - 1:00 PM	Lunch & Rest (Enjoy a Nourishing Meal, Relax, Walk Outside)
1:00 PM - 2:30 PM	Deep Focus Work (Customized Applications, Portfolio Work, Job Research)
2:30 PM - 2:45 PM	Short Break (Listen to Music, Step Outside)
2:45 PM - 4:00 PM	Networking & Outreach (Emails, Coffee Chats, Informational Interviews)
4:00 PM - 5:00 PM	Personal Development (Reading, Podcasts, Learning a New Skill)
5:00 PM - 6:30 PM	Evening Routine & Wind Down (Light Yoga, Reflection, Gratitude Practice)
6:30 PM - 7:30 PM	Dinner & Connection Time (Family, Friends, Hobbies)
7:30 PM - 9:00 PM	Relaxation & Unwinding (TV, Music, Creative Activities, Self-Care)
9:00 PM - 10:00 PM	Sleep Preparation (Limit Screen Time, Deep Breathing, Relaxing Rituals)

Overcoming Anxiety & Self-Doubt

☑ **Recognize Imposter Syndrome:** Self-doubt may creep in, but remember that your skills and experience are still valuable.

☑ **Focus on What You Can Control:** Shift your attention and energy toward actions like networking, upskilling, and applying for jobs helps restore a sense of agency and reduces feelings of helplessness.

☑ **Celebrate Progress:** Track your small wins to reinforce a positive mindset and builds resilience.

ACTION STEP: List three skills or strengths that make you a strong candidate.

Seeking Mental Health & Peer Support

☑ **Lean on Your Support System:** Friends, family, and mentors can offer perspective and encouragement.

☑ **Join Career Transition & Support Groups:** Engaging with others in similar situations can provide motivation and insights.

☑ **Consider Professional Help:** Therapy, career coaching, or mental health resources can help navigate challenges.

ACTION STEP: Identify **one** support resource (peer group, mentor, or professional service) and reach out this week.

How to Rebuild Confidence

Make a list of past career wins, no matter how small.

Identify **three** skills that made you successful in previous roles.

Ask former colleagues for feedback to highlight strengths you may not recognize.

Shift Your Mindset & Own Your Narrative

☑ **Reframe the Layoff:** Treat the layoff as a career pivot—an opening to realign with new opportunities and priorities.

☑ **Recognize the Lessons:** Reflect on the skills, insights, and growth you gained from your previous role.

☑ **Control the Narrative:** When sharing your story, emphasize your strengths, adaptability, and the steps you're taking to move forward.

PRO TIP: Use the Bridge Formula to Own Your Transition

- Start with a defining moment (like your layoff).
- Connect it to relevant skills.
- Share one proactive step you've taken.
- End with your vision for your next role.

Sample Narrative:

"Being laid off as a Customer Success Manager reinforced my passion for solving client challenges and optimizing processes. During my transition, I earned a Lean Six Sigma certification to deepen my expertise in operational efficiency. Now, I'm excited to apply my problem-solving skills and customer-first mindset in a project management role, where I can help teams streamline workflows and drive meaningful results."

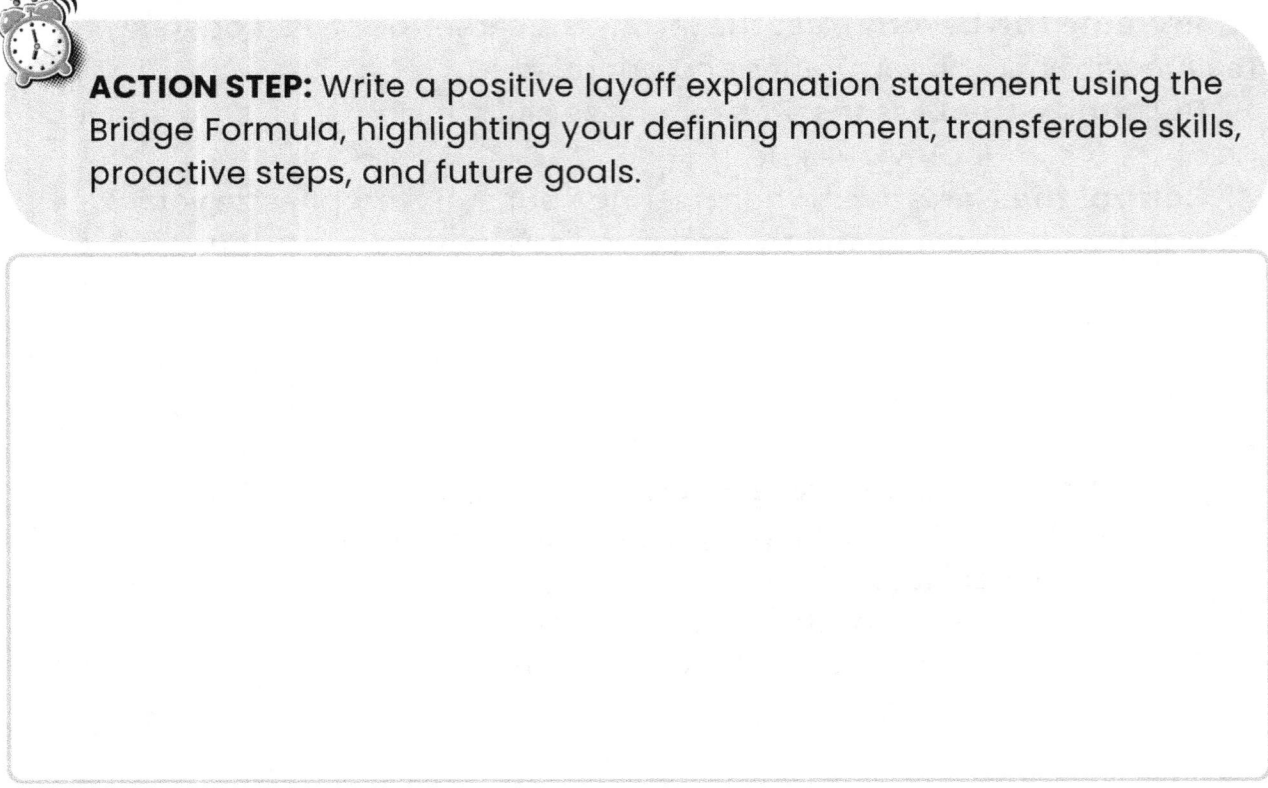

ACTION STEP: Write a positive layoff explanation statement using the Bridge Formula, highlighting your defining moment, transferable skills, proactive steps, and future goals.

Reframe Negative Self-Talk with Empowering Language

Your internal dialogue shapes how you present yourself to future employers and your network. Instead of dwelling on job loss, reframe the experience in a way that reinforces your value.

✕ Self-Doubt Thought	☑ Empowering Reframe
"I was let go because I wasn't good enough."	"My role was impacted by restructuring, but my expertise in [key skills] is still valuable and in demand."
"Nobody will want to hire me now."	"I bring [years] of experience in [industry], and I'm actively seeking the right opportunity to make an impact."
"I don't know how to talk about my layoff."	"The layoff was beyond my control, but I'm using this time to refocus and find a role that aligns with my strengths, skills and values."

AI Prompt: Rewrite Limiting Beliefs as Empowering Statements

"Please reframe these thoughts I'm having after my layoff: **[Insert 2–3 beliefs or phrases]**. I want to sound more confident and grounded when talking to others."

ACTION STEP: Choose **one** limiting belief you've had about your layoff and rewrite it as an empowering statement. Say it out loud or write it down where you'll see it daily.

Confidence Starts Before You Feel Ready

Confidence rarely shows up before action, but it often arrives because of it. The more you move, even in small ways, the more grounded you become in your value.

Try one of these small steps to build momentum:
- Practice saying your elevator pitch aloud while on a walk.
- Share your career goals with one trusted friend.
- Reflect on a win from your last role, and write it down.

Daily Check-In Tracker

Purpose: To create a mindful routine that fosters small daily wins and emotional awareness during recovery.

Date	How am I feeling today?	What's one small win?	What's my best next step?

ACTION STEP: Fill this out each morning or evening. Over time, you'll notice patterns, progress, and opportunities for gentle self-correction.

Final Thoughts

Navigating a layoff can feel disorienting, but your emotions are valid, and you're not alone in them. Prioritizing your well-being isn't a pause from progress; it's the foundation for it. Clarity returns when you care for yourself. Confidence is rebuilt through small, consistent choices, mindset shifts, and support systems that remind you who you are beyond the job. The role will come. But reclaiming your sense of self—that's where true recovery begins.

Family Communication Guidance: Navigating Conversations About a Layoff

A layoff can shift the dynamics at home, bringing new pressures and emotions. You may feel the urge to appear strong or shield loved ones from your worries, but honest, age-appropriate communication builds trust, support, and shared resilience. The following scripts and action steps are designed to help you navigate these conversations with clarity and calm—even when emotions run high.

Talking to Your Partner

✏️ **Reflection Prompt:**
- How do I want my family to feel during this transition?
- What message matters most in how I show up with them?

☑️ **Be Transparent but Reassuring:** Share the situation honestly while focusing on proactive steps you're taking.
☑️ **Discuss Financial Adjustments:** Align on budgeting, short-term priorities, and potential income streams.
☑️ **Acknowledge Emotional Impact:** Layoffs affect both partners emotionally—support each other through uncertainty.

ACTION STEP: Schedule a time to discuss financial planning and job search strategies together.

Communicating with Children

☑ **Keep It Age-Appropriate:** Younger children need reassurance of stability, while older children may understand financial shifts.

☑ **Frame It as a Transition, Not a Crisis:** Explain that this is a temporary phase and that you're working toward new opportunities. See sample scripts on page 77.

☑ **Encourage Openness:** Let them ask questions and express their feelings.

JOB SEEKER SPOTLIGHT

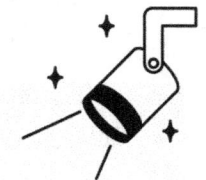

Building Trust Through a Candid Conversation

Briana, a Florida-based administrative professional, wasn't sure how to explain her layoff to her 8-year-old son. She worried it might cause unnecessary fear or confusion. But when she calmly shared that her job had ended and that the family would be making some changes together, his response surprised her—he met her honesty with empathy, and even curiosity.

"I thought I had to protect him from everything. But giving him just enough truth made him feel included and safe."

Takeaway: Age-appropriate honesty doesn't burden children—it helps them feel secure. Even young kids can handle change better when they're trusted with simple truths.

Scripts for Communicating About a Layoff to Children

Young Children (Ages 4-8) – Keep It Simple & Reassuring

"I'm not going to work at the same place anymore, but everything will be okay. I'm looking for a new job that will be even better. In the meantime, we'll spend more time together, and you can help me with little things while I figure out what's next!"

Preteens (Ages 9-12) – Provide More Context But Stay Optimistic

"You might hear me talking about finding a new job because my company had to make some changes, and I won't be working there anymore. It wasn't because I did anything wrong—it's just something that happens sometimes. I'm using this as a chance to find something even better. Things might be a little different for a while, but we're making a plan so that everything is okay."

Teenagers (Ages 13-18) – Be Honest, Practical, and Engage in Problem-Solving

"I want to share something important with you. I was recently laid off from my job because the company had to make some changes. This doesn't mean I did anything wrong—it just means I need to find something new. It's a stressful time, but I'm working on solutions, and I'd love for us to work together as a family to make this transition smoother. If you have any questions or concerns, I want to hear them."

ACTION STEP: Plan a simple, age-appropriate conversation with your child or children about the layoff, focusing on reassurance, stability, and optimism for what's ahead.

Addressing Extended Family & Friends

☑ **Share on Your Terms:** You don't owe anyone every detail. Share what feels right with those you trust—whether they're relatives or chosen family.

☑ **Set Boundaries if Needed:** If certain conversations feel overwhelming or unhelpful, it's okay to steer them toward encouragement or redirect entirely.

☑ **Ask for Help When Necessary:** upport can take many forms—job leads, childcare, or simply someone to listen. Reach out to those who truly have your back, whether they're relatives or trusted friends. Not everyone deserves a front-row seat to your journey.

PRO TIP: You don't need to share everything all at once. It's okay to communicate in layers, starting with what feels safe and manageable. As your situation evolves and your confidence grows, you can revisit the conversation and share more when you're ready. Give yourself permission to set the pace.

Scripts for Communicating About a Layoff to Adults

*"Hey **[Family/Friend's Name]**, I wanted to share something with you before you heard it elsewhere. Recently, my role at **[Company Name]** was impacted due to **[reason—e.g., company restructuring, downsizing, economic conditions]**, and I'm no longer with the company.*

This was unexpected, and it's tough to go through a change like this. However, I'm choosing to see this as an opportunity to reassess what's next for me and take intentional steps forward. I'm also being mindful of my well-being, so I'm balancing job searching with self-care.

*If you hear of opportunities in **[your field/industry]** or know someone I should connect with, I'd appreciate an introduction. More than anything, I just appreciate your support and encouragement as I navigate this transition.*

Thanks for being in my corner—it really means a lot."

ACTION STEP: Identify key people to inform and determine how much detail you feel comfortable sharing.

Addressing Unsupportive Family About Your Layoff

Navigating conversations about your layoff with family can be challenging, especially when their reactions are unsupportive, dismissive, or anxiety-inducing. Some family members may unintentionally undermine your confidence, equate job loss with personal failure, or pressure you into rushing decisions. It's important to set boundaries, reframe negative narratives, and communicate in a way that preserves your peace and confidence while managing their concerns. The key is to stay focused on your plan, reinforce your value, and redirect the conversation toward productive discussions.

> *"I wanted to share a quick update. I was recently laid off from my job at **[Company Name]** due to **[company restructuring, downsizing, or leave this vague if necessary]**. It's an adjustment, but I'm handling it.*
>
> *I don't want to dwell on it too much, as I'm focusing on moving forward. I appreciate your concern, but I'm managing things in a way that works for me.*
>
> *Right now, I'm taking this time to explore my next steps, and I'd rather focus on solutions than the past. If anything changes, I'll update you when I'm ready."*

If They Keep Pushing, Set a Firm Limit:
"I know you might have opinions, but what I need most right now is space to figure things out on my own. Let's talk about something else."

Exit Strategy (If They Keep Pressuring You):
"I appreciate you checking in, but I don't want to keep talking about this. Let's move on to something else."

Final Thoughts

Family and close relationships can be a source of strength, but not always. It depends on the dynamics. Sometimes, a healthy distance is what allows you to protect your peace and focus on healing. When support is available, honest, age-appropriate communication can foster understanding, reduce stress, and help everyone adjust together. Start with just one meaningful conversation—it has the power to shift the tone of your home or your heart.

PHASE 2
Rebuilding Career Confidence

Rediscover Your Career Drivers
After a Layoff

In the rush to find the next job, it's easy to overlook the deeper opportunity a layoff presents. This season of transition can be a powerful moment to pause, reflect, and realign your career with what truly matters—your values, strengths, and long-term goals. Rediscovering what drives you can help you move forward with renewed purpose and a stronger sense of direction.

☑ **Reflect on Your Strengths & Achievements:** What tasks leave you feeling energized? Which accomplishments are you most proud of? These insights highlight the skills you naturally lean into and enjoy using.

☑ **Assess What You Want to Change:** Were there aspects of your previous job—tasks, culture, schedule—that no longer supported your career goals or lifestyle? Identifying what no longer fits helps you avoid repeating patterns.

☑ **Prioritize Job Satisfaction Factors:** What does job satisfaction look like for you now? Consider factors like flexibility, work-life harmony, compensation, leadership opportunities, and company culture when envisioning your next role.

Once you've identified what energizes and drains you, go deeper: What values guide your choices? What matters most in how, where, and why you work?

Use the **Career Drivers Map Worksheet** on page 94 to capture your reflections. Look for patterns that reveal what truly drives your fulfillment and motivation.

☑ **Explore Industries & Businesses That Align With Your Interests & Values:** Which industries or organizations reflect your values, spark curiosity, or inspire you, beyond just the job title? When your work aligns with what you care about, career satisfaction becomes more sustainable and meaningful.

ACTION STEP: Name the **three** career elements that matter most right now, then let them guide your next decision.

Align Your Career Path With Your Core Values

☑ **Define Your Professional Values:** Do you value creativity, routine, autonomy, collaboration, impact, or stability? Knowing this will guide your next steps.

☑ **Use Past Experiences as a Guide:** Identify patterns in past roles that brought fulfillment or frustration to refine your career direction.

☑ **Ensure Career Fit:** Research ndustries and roles that align with your core values and long-term aspirations.

ACTION STEP: List **five** values that define how you want to work and compare them to your target job or industry.

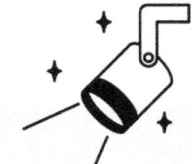

Reclaiming Purpose Through Reflection

After being laid off from a high-pressure tech role, **Elaine,** a Tennessee-based project manager, felt drained and directionless. Rather than rushing into another full-time job, she gave herself space to reflect. She took a career values assessment and began journaling daily about her peak experiences—the moments at work when she felt most energized, effective, and fulfilled.

A pattern emerged: she thrived when helping others make sense of complex problems. That insight led her to start a part-time coaching practice for professionals in transition, while also doing fractional project work in knowledge management.

Today, Elaine's work aligns with both her strengths and her energy. Her story is a reminder that rebuilding your career doesn't have to mean returning the same way you left.

Takeaway: Sometimes the clearest next step isn't another job but a smarter, more sustainable way of working.

Elaine didn't just reflect; she took strategic action. In the same way, you can explore roles that align with your strengths and values, even if they look different from what you've done before.

Explore Career Options That Align With Your Strengths

☑️ **Assess Your Transferable Skills:** Identify how your existing skills can be applied across industries, not just in your current field.

☑️ **Look Beyond Job Titles:** Focus on the actual work functions, challenges and environments that align with your strengths and interests.

☑️ **Test New Career Paths:** Use freelance projects, contract roles, or volunteering as low-risk ways to explore new fields before making a full transition.

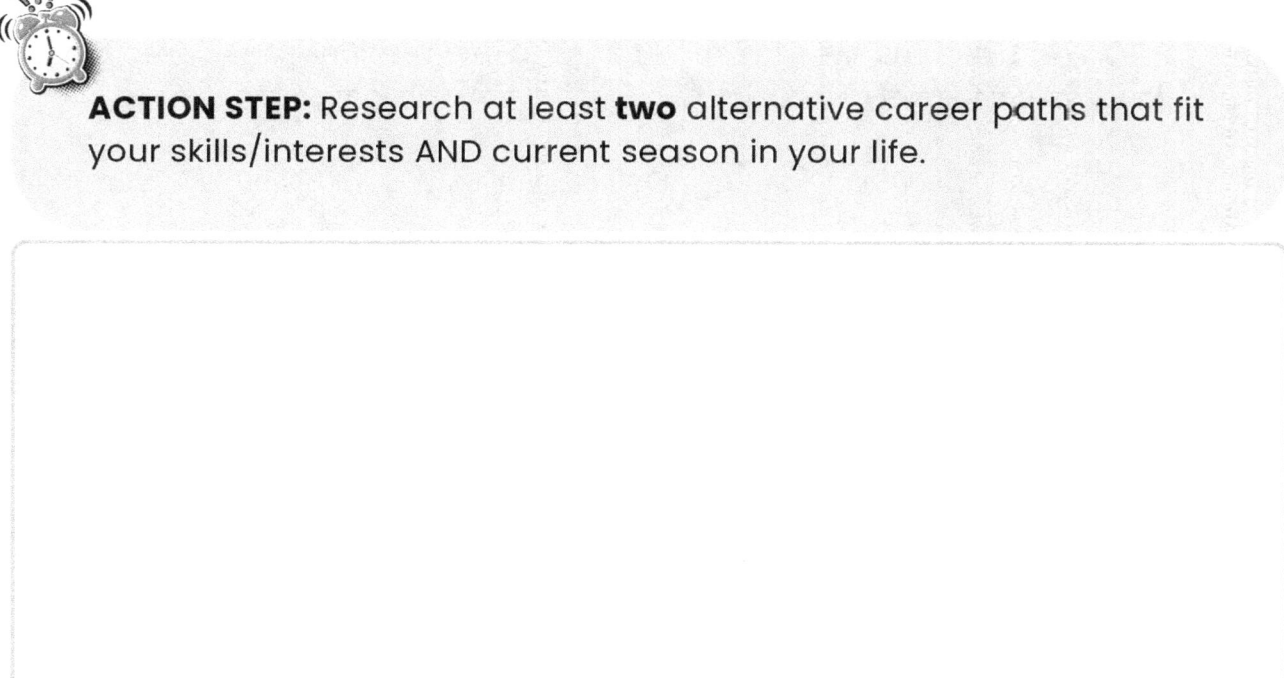

ACTION STEP: Research at least **two** alternative career paths that fit your skills/interests AND current season in your life.

If you're still unsure how your strengths and values translate into real roles, you're not alone. AI-powered platforms (like O*NET, LinkedIn Career Explorer, or VMock) and guided career assessments can help you map your skills to in-demand roles, discover emerging fields, and uncover new possibilities you may not have thought to explore.

Not Sure Where Your Skills Lead? Let Data and AI Help

If you're feeling unsure about how your strengths translate into real roles, you're not alone. Fortunately, smart tools can offer clarity and direction.

☑ AI-Powered Career Insights

Tools like LinkedIn Career Explorer, ChatGPT, Talentprise, and TeoChat's Career Coach GPT analyze your background and goals to suggest tailored career paths, highlight transferable skills, and identify potential gaps—all using real-time labor market data.

☑ Personality & Career Assessments

Platforms like CliftonStrengths, Holland Code (RIASEC), Truity, and Sokanu help you align your strengths, interests, and work style with roles that truly fit.

PRO TIP: Use tools like Claude AI to ask follow-up questions based on your results (e.g., *"How can an ENFP thrive in remote team leadership?"*).

☑ Stay Ahead with Industry Trends

Explore fast-growing fields like AI, clean energy, and digital health. Platforms such as Bing AI, Eightfold.ai, and Coursera's AI Coach can help you research certifications, uncover skill adjacencies, and build future-proof skills.

Additional AI Tools to Consider

Category	Tools	Key Features
Resume & Interview Prep	VMock, HireAI	AI resume scoring, mock interviews with recruiter-style feedback
Networking	LinkedIn AI Assistant, Beamery	Suggests key connections and refines outreach messages
Job Search	Indeed AI, Arc's HireAI	Matches you to roles using real-time job data and LLMs
Portfolios	KickResume AI	Helps career changers build portfolios that showcase transferable skills

ACTION STEPS:
- Run a Holland Code test, then ask ChatGPT to explore niche roles like *"AI ethics specialist"* or *"circular economy consultant."*
- Ask Bing AI(Microsoft Copilot): *"What emerging roles in healthcare align with my project management experience?"*
- Use your preferred AI tool to optimize your resume for hybrid roles and applicant tracking systems (ATS).

PRO TIP: AI tools are powerful, but pairing them with human mentors or career coaches can offer the nuance and perspective needed for complex decisions.

Making Sense Of These Insights

Now that you've identified your key skills, values, and interests, it's time to connect the dots and craft a clear, compelling career direction. This step helps you spot patterns, find alignment, and articulate what truly drives you in your next role.

How to Stitch It Together

Look for Overlapping Themes: What common threads show up across your strengths, interests, and values? Are certain roles, industries, or challenges calling to you?

Define Your Professional Identity: Consider how your skills solve meaningful problems. What unique lens or lived experience do you bring to the table?

Draft a Career Narrative Statement (2–3 sentences):
- What kind of work lights you up?
- What impact do you want to make?
- What environments help you thrive?

AI Prompt: Clarify My Career Drivers

"Help me identify the common themes in my favorite past roles or projects. I want to better understand what motivates me and which types of roles might align with that.
 Include in your input:
- 2–3 past roles or projects you enjoyed
- What you liked about them (e.g., solving problems, collaborating, working independently)
- The impact you had (e.g., improved a process, supported a team, helped customers)"

Need Help Crafting Your Career Narrative? Start Here.
Use this simple reflection framework to get your thoughts flowing:
- *"I feel strongest when I'm..."*
- *"I've used this strength to..."*
- *"I'm most fulfilled in roles that..."*

Once you've completed those prompts, combine your responses into a short career narrative—something you can use in interviews, on LinkedIn, and even in your resume summary.

Example Career Narrative:
"Solving complex challenges through data-driven strategy and process improvement is where I thrive. With a strong focus on operational efficiency and seamless customer experiences, I turn scattered efforts into structured solutions that get results. Known for contributing in collaborative, fast-paced environments, I'm energized by innovation, continuous learning, and outcomes that drive measurable impact."

 **ACTION STEP:** Use AI tools like Perplexity/ ChatGPT/ Gemini/ Copilot/ Claude to refine your statement.

This personalized statement can serve as your guiding compass—shaping your job search, strengthening your elevator pitch, and aligning your LinkedIn profile with roles that truly fit.

 AI Prompt: Career Narrative

"Based on my skills in **[X]**, my values in **[Y]**, and my interest in **[Z]**, generate a polished career narrative that positions me for roles in **[industry/role]**."

Once refined, this statement can guide your job search, shape your elevator pitch, and strengthen your LinkedIn summary—ensuring everything aligns with the opportunities that you want to pursue.

Let Go, Carry Forward

A reflection to help you release what no longer fits and reclaim what still matters.

In the wake of a layoff or major career shift, it's normal to feel untethered. You may find yourself clinging to parts of your old professional identity that no longer support where you're headed, while overlooking the strengths and values still deeply rooted in who you are.

This reflection invites you to make peace with what's behind you—and move forward with intention. Let go of what no longer serves, and carry forward the pieces that still energize and empower your next chapter.

✍ Reflective Prompts

What part of your old career identity no longer fits?
(Consider outdated titles, work environments, beliefs, or habits that limit your growth.)

_____
_____
_____

What lessons did those experiences teach you? (Pull the insight, not the baggage.)

_____
_____
_____

What parts of your career history still reflect your core strengths, values, or energy? (These are the threads you want to carry forward with purpose.)

_____
_____
_____

How do you want to show up next? (Write a short identity statement for your next chapter—for example: "I'm stepping into roles that value clarity, collaboration, and thoughtful leadership.")

_____
_____
_____

📝 Reflection Table

🚫 Let Go What no longer fits	✅ Carry Forward What still energizes and empcwers you
"Chasing titles that drain me"	"Leading with clarity and presence"
"Belief that I must prove my worth constantly"	"Knowing my value is already earned"
"Pace that burned me out"	"Work aligned with my energy rhythms"

Career Drivers Map Worksheet

Your personal compass for what matters most right now

Before moving forward, take a moment to reflect on what truly drives you— your energy, values, work style, and preferences.

Use this worksheet to capture what matters most in this season of your career. It's your personal compass, helping you spot patterns and align with opportunities that fit, not just fill space.

Fill in each section honestly. Highlight anything that surprises you or shows up more than once—you'll use these insights to guide your next steps.

Energizing Tasks

Think about past roles, volunteer work, or life experiences where you felt most engaged.

Tasks that give me energy:

- _____
- _____
- _____

Draining Tasks

These might deplete you, feel like a slog, or drain motivation, even if you're good at them.

Tasks that drain me:

- _____
- _____
- _____

Core Values

What beliefs or principles must be present in your next role or workplace?

My non-negotiable values:

- _____
- _____
- _____

My Ideal Work Style & Structure

Work Style or Focus	Description	☑
Independent Contributor	autonomy, focused tasks, minimal meetings	☐
Collaborative / Team-Based	brainstorming, co-creating, ongoing communication	☐
Managerial	people leadership, mentoring, accountability for others	☐
Non-Managerial	deep expertise, execution, minimal direct reports	☐
Project-Based Work	variety, time-bound, cross-functional	☐
Process-Oriented Work	consistency, clarity, structured tasks	☐
Strategic / Visionary	big-picture thinking, goal setting, innovation	☐
Operational / Execution-Focused	making things run, getting things done	☐

I'm most open to these formats because _____
_____
_____

Skills I Love to Use
These aren't just what you're good at—they're what you enjoy applying.
🔥 Skills I want to use more often:

- _____
- _____
- _____

Industries or Mission Areas That Excite Me
What types of organizations or causes are you drawn to?
🌐 Industries/causes that interest me:

- _____
- _____
- _____

Quick Reflection: What Patterns Do I Notice?

Where do themes repeat across categories? What surprises you?

🖊 Notes:

Final Thoughts

This season is less about returning to who you were and more about evolving into the next version of your professional identity. By reconnecting with your energy, values, and strengths, you can design work that doesn't just fit, but fuels your future.

Even in urgency, you still have choices. And what comes next can be shaped with intention.

Discover What You Do Best
and Where It Can Lead

You bring more to the table than any one title or role can capture. This chapter is about reconnecting with the skills, strengths, and experiences that have always fueled your impact—regardless of industry, level, or job market.

Whether you're preparing for quick reentry, exploring a strategic pivot, or seeking a mix of both, understanding what you do best allows you to:
- Broaden your opportunities across industries
- Speak with clarity and confidence about your value
- Direct your energy toward roles aligned with your strengths and goals

Next, you'll identify your transferable skills and learn how to position them powerfully in today's evolving job landscape.

Skill Mapping: Understand What You Bring—and Where It Can Take You

When you're exploring new roles, clearly understanding and translating your skills can open new doors. Skill mapping helps you identify what's transferable, what's specialized, and what might need updating to align with future opportunities.

Skill Category	Definition
Durable Skills	Long-lasting, foundational skills like communication, leadership, and critical thinking that remain relevant across roles and industries.
Perishable Skills	Skills that require regular updating due to changing technologies or standards—such as specific software, tools, or certifications.
Industry-Specific Skills	Specialized knowledge required in certain fields, such as healthcare compliance or renewable energy regulations.

Skill Translation Table

Current Industry	Transferable Durable Skills	Target Industry	Required Industry-Specific Skills
Retail Management	Team Leadership, Conflict Resolution	Healthcare	Patient Care Protocols, HIPAA Basics
Marketing	Data Analysis, Storytelling	Renewable Energy	Sustainability Reporting, ESG Metrics

Real-World Examples of Transferable Skills

From	To	Transferable Skill Application
Project Management	Operations Management	Managing timelines, budgets, and resources translates directly to workflow optimization and resource planning
Customer Service/Experience	Sales/Account Management	Building rapport and resolving issues supports client retention and revenue generation
Marketing	Business Development	Audience targeting and storytelling support strategic growth and outreach efforts
Teaching	Corporate Training/Instructional Design	Lesson planning and facilitating learning transfer smoothly into training roles
Data Entry	Data Analysis	Working with large datasets builds accuracy and comfort with data tools—critical in business intelligence roles

JOB SEEKER SPOTLIGHT

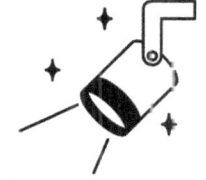

Transferable Skills in Action

After being laid off from a large retail chain, **Jordan,** a store operations manager with over a decade of experience, knew they needed a fresh start. Healthcare had always intrigued them, but they weren't sure how their background in scheduling, crisis management, and inventory oversight would be seen outside of retail.

Using LinkedIn's Career Explorer, Jordan mapped their skil s to roles in hospital operations and patient services. The overlap surprised them: team leadership, logistics coordination, and vendor management were all critical in healthcare environments, too.

Jordan took a free online course in healthcare systems basics and reached out to a former employee who had transitioned into t¬e field. That connection led to a conversation—and a referral—for a temp role in hospital supply coordination.

Eight months later, that temporary position turned into a full-time offer. Jordan now supports daily logistics for a regional hospital, bringing structure and calm to fast-moving environments.

Takeaway: A career pivot doesn't always require starting over. When you connect the dots between what you've done and where you want to go, transferable skills can become your strongest asset.

AI + Assessment Tools to Power Your Pivot
Use These Strategically:

- O*NET OnLine: Explore detailed skill and task requirements for roles across industries.
- SkillScan: Helps you identify your strongest transferable skills through guided assessments.
- ChatGPT / Claude / Gemini / Co-Pilot: Use AI prompts to translate your past experience into language aligned with target roles.
- Eightfold.ai / Skillsyncer: Analyze your resume against job descriptions and discover skill adjacencies.

 AI Prompt: Skill Mapping

"Help me translate my experience in **[current role]** to skills needed for **[target role]**. Highlight transferable strengths and suggest language for my resume."

Future-Proofing Your Skills

As industries evolve, so do the skills they require. The best strategy? Pair your durable strengths and interests with emerging needs.

☑ Durable Skills to Prioritize

- Critical Thinking
- Cross-Cultural Communication
- Resilience

⚠ Perishable Skills to Monitor

- Generative AI Tools (e.g., ChatGPT, Midjourney)
- ESG & Sustainability Reporting

📚 Suggested Learning Resources

- Coursera: Generative AI for Everyone
- LinkedIn Learning: Sustainability Fundamentals

PRO TIPS:

☑ **Adopt a hybrid learning mindset:** Combine what you already do well with emerging knowledge that's gaining traction in your field.

☑ **Use AI & Assessment Tools Strategically:** Platforms like O*NET, SkillScan, and ChatGPT can help you uncover hidden skill overlaps, explore alternative career paths, and generate language to position your experience effectively.

☑ **Analyze Job Descriptions Like a Translator:** Look for patterns in the most in-demand skills across roles you're targeting. Then, match them to your experience—even if the terminology differs. Use tools like Skillsyncer or LinkedIn Skills Insights to guide your alignment.

☑ **Cross-Check with Your Values:** It's not just about what you can do, but what energizes and fulfills you. As you explore roles, ask: Do these environments and responsibilities reflect what matters most to me now?

AI Prompt: Skill Mapping

"Generate a categorized list of my durable, industry-specific, and transferable skills based on my previous role as **[your job title]**. Highlight the top 5 most relevant skills for transitioning into **[target role or industry]**."

Optional: Include examples of past projects or goals to make the AI response more tailored and actionable.

JOB SEEKER SPOTLIGHT

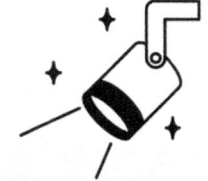

Strengths in a New Light

After a departmental restructure led to her layoff, **Janelle** faced a decision: leave the organization altogether or explore internal opportunities that offered more alignment. Despite being close to retirement, she had no intention of slowing down. With the rising cost of living and a strong desire to keep contributing meaningfully, she paused to reflect on what truly energized her.

Though she had worked in administrative support for over a decade, what she really loved was helping others gain clarity, solve problems, and grow their confidence. After completing a strengths assessment, Janelle identified an opening in a nearby department and proposed her value-add for a newly created Support Specialist role.

It wasn't a vertical promotion, but it was a strategic lateral move that gave her more energy, visibility, and peace. The new role allowed her to coach new hires, lead systems training, and contribute in ways that honored her strengths, interests and values.

Takeaway: Not all promotions go upward. Sometimes the smartest move is lateral—one that protects your energy, aligns with your values, and builds range in ways that matter more than a title.

102

Skill Development Planner

Not every career pivot requires brand-new skills. Often, your existing strengths are exactly what's needed—but sharpening just one can give you a competitive edge. Use this planner to take one skill and develop it intentionally through a blend of education, experience, and exposure.

Skill	Education (Course/ Resource)	Experience (Project Idea)	Exposure (Mentorship/ Networking)	Timeline (Start/ Complete)

PRO TIPS:
- Focus on one core skill to sharpen.
- Strengthen through a blend of Education (courses), Experience (projects), and Exposure (mentorship, networking, shadowing).
- Prioritize real-work application.
- Record your learning from this experience.

ACTION STEP: Where can you apply or test this skill in a low-stakes environment? Look for stretch opportunities—like a volunteer project, side gig, pilot initiative, or cross-functional collaboration—that let you learn through doing without the pressure of perfection.

Final Thoughts

Every skill you've developed, strength you've honed, and experience you've navigated has shaped the foundation for what comes next. This chapter is about identifying what you do best and using it with intention. When you view your strengths not just as qualifications, but as catalysts, new paths begin to open. Your next move starts with what you already know—and the courage to use it in new ways.

Strengthen Your Job Search Strategy

A successful job search is about resumes and job boards but, most importantly, alignment and informed decision-making. The best opportunities are the ones that reflect your values, leverage your strengths, and support your growth. In this chapter, you'll take a proactive approach to identifying target employers, evaluating opportunities beyond the surface, and balancing both risks and rewards. The goal? To help you focus your energy on the right roles, not just available ones, and make confident, well-informed career moves.

Enhanced Company Evaluation
Red Flags, Green Flags, and Prioritized Insights
A fulfilling, secure career move depends on more than finding a well-written job description. Evaluating potential employers with both curiosity and discernment helps you make choices aligned with your values and priorities. This framework blends proactive research, prioritized insights, and a balanced view of red and green flags.

Step 1: Conduct Proactive Company Research
Before applying, explore multiple sources to build a well-rounded view of each company:

- **Press Releases & News Mentions**

Search "**[Company Name]** + news" or explore Crunchbase/Seeking Alpha for updates like product launches, mergers, or financial results.
Insight: Track key events and assess financial stability.

- **Social Media & Hashtags**

Search hashtags like #LifeAt**[Company]** or #WeAre**[Company]** for insights on employee sentiment and workplace culture.
Insight: Real-time snapshots of employee experience and company values.

- **Executive Interviews or Podcasts**

Look for CEO or founder interviews on YouTube or industry podcasts to understand the company's long-term vision.
Insight: Leadership tone, priorities, and strategic direction.

- **Employee Reviews**

Platforms like Glassdoor, Comparably, and Blind offer insider views on management, growth opportunities, and everyday culture.
Insight: On-the-ground experiences and potential warning signs.

PRO TIP: Cross-reference across sources. Press releases highlight the polished surface; employee reviews reveal what may be beneath.

Step 2: Identify and Scrutinize Red Flags

Red flags aren't deal-breakers by default, but consistent patterns should prompt further investigation. Evaluate each in context and consider your priorities.

Red Flag	What It Might Signal	Severity & Notes
High Turnover Rates	Poor leadership, burnout, unclear expectations	High (especially within key departments)
Negative Employee Reviews	Toxic culture, misaligned values, unclear roles	Medium to High—focus on themes and recency
Lack of Career Advancement	Limited growth, poor investment in talent	Medium—unless growth is a priority for you
Frequent Restructuring	Instability, financial pressure, lack of vision	Medium to High—check for patterns over time

PRO TIP: Match red flags to your personal deal-breakers. If stability is critical, weigh restructuring more heavily. If growth matters most, look closely at advancement signals.

Step 3: Look for Green Flags (Mitigating Factors)

These signals can balance or even outweigh potential red flags, especially when they align with your core values or current season of life:

Green Flag	What It Suggests	Why It Matters
Culture Initiatives	Community involvement, ERGs	Purposeful workplaces often retain talent
Learning & Development	Training, mentorship, tuition support	Growth opportunities even if the role isn't a stretch, i.e., is very similar to roles you've held in the past
Transparent Communication	Regular updates, clear leadership access	Builds trust and reduces uncertainty
Mission Alignment	Resonance with company goals	Drives meaning, motivation, and belonging

Step 4: Conduct a Risk–Reward Assessment

No opportunity is perfect, but a clear-eyed evaluation of trade-offs can help you make empowered decisions.

Ask yourself:

- Where am I willing to compromise? (e.g., longer commute for more autonomy)
- What upside is worth the risk? (e.g., a startup-like company energy in exchange for less structure)
- Do the risks and rewards align with my values and current priorities?

Step 5: Identify and Engage Target Employers

With your priorities clear and research tools in hand, it's time to narrow your focus and take intentional action.

Start by building a shortlist of 5-7 companies that genuinely interest you. These could be organizations whose missions inspire you, whose growth you want to be a part of, or whose work cultures align with how you thrive.

As you evaluate each company, consider:

- Their stated mission, values, and workplace culture
- Adaptability to remote/hybrid work
- How they're responding to industry shifts like AI and automation
- Recent news, product launches, or executive changes
- Growth potential in areas that match your skills and goals

Look for more than just brand names—look for alignment with your values, your current season of life, and the kind of contribution you want to make next.

ACTION STEP: Begin engaging with your shortlist—follow them on LinkedIn, connect with employees, and tailor your applications to reflect the research and resonance you've built.

You've narrowed your focus and identified where you'd love to work. Now, it's time to dig deeper—gather intel, understand what employers are really looking for, and tailor how you present yourself across every platform and conversation.

Step 6: Use Smart Research Tools to Your Advantage

Effective research doesn't need to take hours; it needs to be focused. Below are key resources that give you access to everything from culture insights to hiring trends.

Top Research Resources

Resource	What It's Good For
LinkedIn	Company pages, job postings, leadership profiles, employee content
Glassdoor	Salary ranges, interview reviews, culture ratings
TheLayoff.com	Alerts on restructuring, downsizing, and morale issues
Company Websites	Leadership bios, mission, product direction, hiring pages
Industry Reports	Trends, forecasts, competitor insights, market growth
Your Network	Direct insight into leadership, team dynamics, and daily reality

ACTION STEP: Channel your inner detective. Grab your notebook and schedule 30 minutes daily as "detective time" to research and track insights on companies and roles.

AI Prompt: For Efficient Research

What are the key things I should know about **[Company Name]**? Using information from the company's **[LinkedIn page, recent news articles, and their official website]** (especially the About, Careers, and Investor Relations sections), summarize its recent hiring trends, company culture, financial performance, and key industry challenges.

Step 7: Understand What They're Looking For
Scan 3–5 job descriptions from your target companies.
- Look for recurring themes:
  - Skills sought (e.g., leadership, collaboration, problem-solving, etc.)
  - Values (e.g., innovation, inclusion, customer-centricity, sustainability)
  - Coded language (e.g., "fast-paced environment" may imply high expectations or long hours; "self-starter" may signal limited support or onboarding; "wear many hats" may mean scope creep or startup culture)
- Ask: *What problems are they trying to solve? How does my background position me to help?*

This analysis becomes your blueprint for tailoring your resume, LinkedIn, outreach, and interviews.

Step 8: Align Your Career Brand
Consistency builds trust. Your resume, LinkedIn, cover letter, and interview responses should reinforce the same core message: the value you bring and why it matters now.

Touchpoint	Tips for Alignment
Resume	Tailor each version using key terms and outcome-driven bullets. (More on this on pages 111-114).
LinkedIn	Use relevant keywords, feature key wins, and engage with content in your space.
Cover Letter	Speak directly to company needs. Be specific, not generic.
Interview	Use the ROAR Method: Result – Objective – Action – Restated Result (See page 144).

 AI Prompt: Refine Your Brand

"Based on this job description and my resume, help me tailor my messaging to highlight my most relevant strengths and skills."
[Upload/copy + paste job description and resume]

🔎 Beyond the Job Boards

Job boards are only one piece of the puzzle. To get a fuller, more candid picture of company culture, employee experience, and leadership behavior, explore platforms like:

- Blind
- Comparably
- Fishbowl
- Vault
- AmbitionBox
- The Muse

Pair this research with direct conversations. Reach out to people inside the company or industry for nuanced insights that online reviews may miss.

✅ Craft a High-Impact Resume (and cover letter if required)

Your resume is a carefully curated highlight reel designed to showcase your most transferable skills, measurable and relevant accomplishments, and highest-impact results, not a job history.

- **Tailor for Keywords:** Scan job descriptions for specific terms (skills, tools, role titles), and embed them naturally throughout your resume. This helps you pass the screening processes used by applicant tracking systems (ATS) and signals clear alignment to hiring managers.
- **Focus on Results, Not Just Tasks:** Avoid generic lines like "coordinated events" or "supported teams." Instead, answer: What changed because of your efforts? Did you improve efficiency? Save time? Enhance service?
- **Mirror the Language of the Industry:** Especially when pivoting to a new field, reflect the terminology of your desired role. If the job title is "Program Manager," use that title (accurately) in your resume and LinkedIn headline. Recruiters often search by title—this helps you show up.
- **Start with a Strong Summary:** Lead with a concise professional summary that captures your core strengths and the value you bring. This acts as your "hook" and sets the tone for the rest of your resume.

From Fluff to Facts: Turning Soft Language into Strong Impact

Even if you're not in a numbers-heavy role, your work likely created measurable results. The key is to ask the right questions. Most contributions can be quantified through time saved, people helped, efficiency gained, or quality improved.

Fluffy Statement: Coordinated logistics for team meetings and leadership events.

Let's Ask:
- How many people attended each meeting or event? 20 people
- How often did these meetings happen? Weekly
- How much time did each manager spend drafting talking points before? 1 hour/week
- After you took over, how long did they spend? 15 minutes/week
- What's the time savings across 5 managers? 5 x 45 minutes = 3.75 hours/week
- Over 1 quarter (12 weeks): **3.75 x 12 = 45 hours saved**

Facts-Based Rewrite: Saved leadership team 45+ hours/quarter by streamlining meeting logistics and implementing a prep checklist across 12 recurring events.

PRO TIP: Can't find a number? Find what changed.
Ask:
- What got better?
- For whom?
- How many?
- How often?
- How long before vs. after?

Even one of these answers can strengthen how you communicate your impact, and make your resume and interviews far more compelling.

Using AI to Elevate Your Resume

AI can be a powerful resume assistant, especially when you know how to direct it. Tools like ChatGPT, Gemini, Claude, Teal, and Resume Worded can help you craft a sharper, more customized resume by:
- Tailoring it to the job: Align your resume with a specific job description using role-specific language and ATS-friendly keywords.
- Rewriting it for impact: Transform task-based bullets into achievement-driven statements with measurable results.
- Framing your experience strategically: Use stronger, more employer-facing language that positions your skills as solutions.

 AI Prompt: Optimize or Refine Your Resume Post-Layoff

Whether you're starting from scratch or refining a solid draft, this prompt will help you align your resume with your next best move:

"I was recently laid off from my role as **[Previous Job Title]** at **[Company Name]** and am now exploring opportunities in **[Target Roles/Industry]**. Please help me optimize my resume to:
- Emphasize relevant experience and quantifiable achievements.
- Highlight transferable skills aligned with my target roles.
- Use clear, results-driven language and industry keywords (ATS-friendly).
- Maintain a clean, concise 1–2 page layout with strong visual impact.
- Acknowledge the layoff gracefully, focusing on the value delivered.

Key Background Info:
- Core skills: **[Insert]**
- Major wins: **[Insert]**
- Industries: **[Insert]**
- Target roles: **[Insert]**

Current Resume Content:
[Paste resume content or key bullet points. Be sure to remove personal details.]"

 AI Prompt: Resume Refinement for Career Pivot

Use this prompt when shifting industries or roles and need help translating your past experience into language that fits where you're headed.

"I'm transitioning from **[Current/Previous Industry or Role]** into **[Target Industry or Role]**. Please help me refine my resume to:
- Emphasize transferable skills and achievements most relevant to the new direction.
- Reframe past roles using language and priorities of the target field.
- Use clear, results-driven phrasing with industry-relevant keywords (ATS-friendly).
- Improve focus, structure, and tone for a 1–2 page resume that feels aligned and compelling."

Key Background Info:
- Current/Previous roles: **[Insert]**
- Target roles/industry: **[Insert]**
- Transferable skills: **[Insert]**
- Major wins: **[Insert]**

Here's my current resume text or bullet points for reference:
[Paste resume content—remove any personal details]"

 AI Prompt: Workforce Re-entry Resume Refresh

Use this prompt when you're returning to the workforce and want to confidently reframe your time away while emphasizing your strengths and readiness.

"I'm re-entering the workforce after a period of focused time away from formal employment and am now pursuing roles in **[Target Industry or Job Titles]**. Please help refine my resume to:
- Strategically position my time away as a period of continued growth, learning, or leadership
- Highlight my prior experience, transferable skills, and core strengths aligned with the roles I'm targeting
- Emphasize measurable impact, relevant outcomes, and professional value
- Optimize for keywords and ATS systems
- Maintain a clean, concise, and visually appealing layout within 1–2 pages

Key Background Info:
Relevant activities during time away: **[e.g., consulting, caregiving, skill-building, community leadership]**
- Previous experience: **[Insert]**
- Target roles: **[Insert]**
- Core strengths: **[Insert]**
- Key achievements: **[Insert]**

Here's my current resume or bullet points for reference:
[Paste resume content—remove any sensitive info]"

Step 9: Activate Your Network
Some of the best opportunities never make it to job boards. Reaching out to your network is powerful.

- Reconnect with former colleagues, mentors, fellow alumni, and friends. Let them know you're exploring new roles and share the type of work you're seeking.
- Be specific in your ask—request introductions, insights on company culture, or intel on upcoming openings.
- Follow and connect with recruiters, especially those in your target industry or companies of interest.

Remember: Many jobs are filled through referrals before they're ever posted. Networking isn't optional but strategic.

Step 10: Tailor Your Applications
Every application should feel like it was written for that role at that company. Customization shows care and gets noticed.

- Map your skills to the job: Make it easy for hiring managers to see how your experience matches what they need.
- Customize each cover letter: Mention company initiatives, reflect back their language, and express authentic enthusiasm for the role.
- Emphasize your versatility: Clearly articulate transferable skills especially when pivoting to a new industry or function.

Step 11: Track Your Applications Strategically
Efficient, targeted tracking helps maintain momentum, prevents overwhelm, and refines your strategy based on real-world insights.

- Simple tracking tools: Use accessible tools such as Trello, Airtable, or even a basic spreadsheet to track roles, application statuses, contacts, and follow-up activities.
- Analyze & adjust: Every few weeks, evaluate your outreach and application responses. Double down on what's working, and fine-tune what's not.
- Structured follow-ups: Maintain a polite, professional tone to keep your candidacy visible without appearing overly aggressive.

AI Prompt: Create a Job Tracker Spreadsheet

"Create a simple spreadsheet layout to help me track job applications, networking conversations, and follow-up actions."

Step 12: Leverage Hidden Market Opportunities
Some of the most rewarding roles are never posted online. They're filled through connections, timing, and proactive outreach. This is the **hidden job market,** and tapping into it gives you a distinct edge.

- Connect strategically on LinkedIn: Use your research to identify professionals at your target companies, especially in departments where you'd like to work.
- Reach out directly: Send a thoughtful message to hiring managers or internal recruiters, even if no role is currently posted. Introduce yourself, express your interest, and share how your background aligns with the team's needs.
- Lead with value: Use what you've learned about the company's goals, challenges, or current initiatives to position yourself not as a job seeker but as a potential solution.

Think like a consultant, not just a candidate. Show how your experience directly addresses their needs—whether it's scaling a team, improving efficiency, launching a project, or driving innovation.

Step 13: Stay Agile and Evaluate Progress
Your job search is a strategy, not a sprint, so adapt as you go.

- Set weekly goals to maintain momentum. For example: 3 tailored applications + 2 networking conversations.
- Every 2–4 weeks, pause to reflect.
  - What's working?
  - What's not?
  - Where are you seeing traction?
- If you hit a plateau, don't push harder. Step back and adjust your strategy.

JOB SEEKER SPOTLIGHT

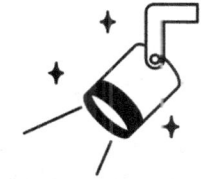

The Power of Industry Relationships

As a Michigan-based category manager at a regional grocery chain, **Serena** was ready for a bigger stage. Instead of starting with applications, she tapped into her industry network:

She reached out to a former vendor contact at a Fortune 500 consumer goods company.

That connection led to a referral and an interview, before the role was publicly posted.

In the interview, she spot ighted her retail insights and history of collaborative wins.

The result? A new role that became a launchpad. Serena eventually moved into corporate sales management at a second Fortune 500 company, building on the foundation of her initial leap.

Takeaway: Don't wait for job boards to shape your path. One relationship, and one well-timed message, can open doors and change your career trajectory.

🔍 Search Less, Find More: Using LinkedIn & Google Strategically

Job postings online often attract hundreds of applicants within hours. To stay ahead, treat LinkedIn and Google like research tools.

🌐 LinkedIn Search Hacks

1. Find Roles Before They're Posted
- **How to:** Use LinkedIn's search bar with smart strings to uncover hidden opportunities.
- **Search String Examples:**
  - "Product Manager" AND ("Hiring" OR "Now Hiring" OR "Expanding Team")
  - ("Data Scientist" OR "Data Analyst") AND ("Openings" OR "Careers")
  - "Software Engineer" AND "Hiring" AND "Austin" (add location if relevant)
- **Filters:** After the initial keyword search, use LinkedIn's built-in filters (date posted, location, experience level, company, etc.) to narrow results.
- **Alerts:** Set up search alerts for your key terms to receive daily or weekly notifications of new posts.

2. Narrow Down Results and Monitor Real-Time Openings
- **Posts:** Click the "Posts" tab to see status updates, hiring announcements, and discussions.
- **Filters:** Use "All Filters" to specify connection level (1st, 2nd, 3rd+), industry, location, and date posted. Focus on "Past Week" to find recent announcements.
- **My Network:** Prioritize posts from your direct connections for warm leads and potential referrals.

3. Identify the Right People for Networking
- **Company Search:** Search for your target company.
- **People Filter:** Click "People" to see a list of employees.
- **Targeted Filtering:** Filter by department, job title, or location to find relevant contacts.
- **Shared Connections:** Look for shared connections to request warm introductions.
- **Advanced Search:** Use LinkedIn Recruiter Lite for advanced filters like skills, experience, and location. It's a paid tool, but new users can access a 30-day free trial.
- **Alumni Tool:** If you attended the same university, use the Alumni tool for shared connections.

4. Engage First, Ask Later (Building Rapport)

- **Thoughtful Engagement:** Comment and like on posts from your target contacts, offering insightful feedback or relevant questions.
- **Personalized Connection Requests:** Send a customized message referencing shared interests or experiences when connecting (avoid generic requests).
- **Follow-Up Strategy:** Engage with their content after connecting before asking for a referral or informational interview.
- **Benefit:** Build familiarity and rapport, increasing the likelihood of a positive response.

 AI Prompt: Search Queries

"Help me generate a list of advanced LinkedIn and Google search queries to uncover hidden job opportunities in **[industry]** for roles like **[target job title]**. I want to find hiring managers, recent announcements, and unlisted job leads."

🌐 Google Search Hacks

Go beyond job boards and use Google strategically to uncover roles and insights.

1. Uncover Roles on Company Sites

- **How to:** Use the site: operator to search directly within a company's website. Combine this with relevant keywords.
- **Search String:** site:companyname.com careers "job title"
- **Example:** site:nike.com careers "supply chain analyst"
- **Refinement:** site:nike.com (careers OR jobs OR "work with us") "supply chain analyst" – include multiple keywords.
- **Benefit:** Find roles not advertised elsewhere, including niche or newly created positions.

2. Find Hiring Trends or Recent Expansions

- **How to:** Identify if a company is growing and actively hiring.
- **Search String:** "Company Name" AND (hiring OR expansion OR new location) AND Year.
- **Example:** "Salesforce" AND (hiring OR expansion OR "new office") AND Year.
- **Time Filter:** Use Google's "Tools" → "Any Time" dropdown to filter results by "Past Month" or "Past Year" for timely information.
- **Benefit:** Focus your efforts on companies with growth potential and expanding teams.

3. Locate Contact Info or Department Leads

- **How to:** Find potential networking contacts or hiring managers.
- Search String: site:linkedin.com/in AND "Job Title" AND "Company Name" AND Location.
- **Example:** site:linkedin.com/in AND "HR Director" AND "Nike" AND "Beaverton, OR"
- **Variations:** Try site:linkedin.com/in AND ("recruiter" OR "talent acquisition") AND "Company Name"
- **Refinement:** Use quotation marks for exact phrases: site:linkedin.com/in AND "Talent Acquisition Manager" AND "Acme Corp"
- **Benefit:** Identify key contacts for networking and informational interviews.

4. Discover Industry Insights and News

- **How to:** Stay informed about industry trends and company news.
- Search String: "Company Name" AND (industry OR trends OR news OR insights)
- **Example:** "General Motors" AND (electric vehicles OR sustainability trends OR news)
- **Google Alerts:** Set up Google Alerts to receive email notifications for specific companies, keywords, or industry trends.
- **Benefit:** Stay up-to-date on market dynamics and potential opportunities.

5. Find Competitor Information

- **How to:** Research competitor landscapes.
- **Search String:** "Company Name" AND (competitors OR "market share" OR "industry analysis")
- **Example:** "Apple" AND (competitors OR "market share" OR "smartphone industry analysis")
- **Benefit:** Prepare for interviews with a deeper understanding of the company's competitive landscape.

6. Refine Your Search with Advanced Operators

- **"" (Quotation Marks):** Search for exact phrases (e.g., "project manager").
- OR: Combine multiple terms (e.g., analyst OR specialist).
- **- (Minus Sign):** Exclude specific terms (e.g., marketing-manager).
- site:: Search within a specific website (e.g., site:linkedin.com).
- filetype:: Search for specific file types (e.g., filetype:pdf "company strategy").

PRO TIP: Save Time with Targeted Search
Tired of endless scrolling on generic job boards? Use the Job Search Database to find hundreds of niche job sites, organized by industry and career field. It's a smarter, faster way to go directly where your ideal roles are posted. Scan the QR code to access the full database and streamline your search.

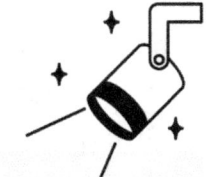

From Scattered to Strategic with the Bullseye Method

After a layoff, **Tracy** jumped into job searching headfirst, but quickly found himself overwhelmed. He was applying to too many roles that didn't fully align with what he really wanted.

Here's how he turned it around:
- ☑ Mapped his ideal job using a bullseye framework:
  - ◎ Center (Ideal): Roles that matched nearly all his preferences—industry, team size, salary, impact, growth.
  - ○ Inner Circle: Strong fits, missing only one or two things.
  - Outer Circle: Roles that were a stretch or fallback.
- ☑ Created a tracker with columns for role title, company, bullseye tier, application date, contact status, and follow-up.
- ☑ Set a weekly cadence: 3 ideal or strong-fit applications + 2 networking messages + 1 review session to reassess.

With his priorities clear and system in place, Tracy stopped wasting time on poor-fit roles. In just over a month, he reached the final round for two roles in his center circle—and ultimately accepted an offer that checked all his top boxes.

Takeaway: Strategy beats speed. The bullseye helped Tracy focus on what mattered most, while the tracker kept him moving forward with intention and clarity.

LinkedIn Message Templates for Strategic Outreach

You've already learned how to identify the right people to contact. Now, here's how to start the conversation, without the awkwardness.

Template #1: For a Posted Role

*Hi **[Name]**, I saw your post about the **[Job Title]** opening. I'm really interested—my experience in **[A]** and **[B]** aligns with what you're looking for, and I'd love to share how I can support **[Team/Project/Goal]**. My resume is attached. When would be a good time to connect?*

Template #2: For a Cold Outreach (No Role Posted Yet)

*Hi **[Name]**, I admire **[Company]**'s recent work in **[specific area]** and wanted to reach out. I noticed **[mention a challenge, initiative, or trend]** and have experience in **[specific skill/expertise]** that could contribute to those efforts. In my last role at **[Company]**, I **[briefly mention relevant achievement]**. While I didn't see a current opening that's an exact match, I'd love to stay in touch and be considered for future opportunities. Would you be open to keeping me in mind or sharing any upcoming hiring needs?*

Template #3: Learn About the Culture

*Hi **[Name]**, I came across your profile while researching **[Company]** and noticed your experience in **[Department/Role]**. I'd love to learn more about what it's like to work there and any insights you might have. Would you be open to a quick, informal chat? No pressure—just looking to connect and learn more!*

Why This Works

✅ Demonstrates that you've done your homework by referencing a real company challenge, initiative, or trend.

✅ Skips the crowded applicant pool and reaches hiring managers directly.

✅ Shows initiative and positions you as a proactive problem-solver.

✅ Keeps the tone low-pressure—you're not asking for a job, just opening the door.

✅ Aligns your skills with business needs—before a role is even posted.

✅ Gets you closer to decision-makers, faster.

In a competitive job market, proactive communication is your edge. Make this a weekly habit to uncover hidden roles and spark valuable conversations.

✒️ **Reflection Prompt:**

What small shift can I make this week to sharpen my approach and increase the impact of my job search strategy?

ACTION STEP: Identify one key insight—something you've learned about what's been missing, misaligned, or overlooked. Then, turn that insight into a specific, achievable goal for the next 7 days.
Example:

- Insight: "I've only been applying passively—I haven't reached out to anyone directly."
- Goal: "I'll send 3 personalized outreach messages to former colleagues or recruiters this week."

Final Thoughts

A job search guided by clarity and intention will always outpace a scattershot approach. In today's market, it's not about how many applications you submit but about how well your actions align with your strengths, values, and goals. Referrals, relationships, and relevance open more doors than cold clicks ever will. Prioritize quality over quantity. Meaningful conversations over mass applications. Stay focused. Stay flexible.

Elevate Your LinkedIn Presence

LinkedIn remains one of the top places recruiters search for talent. It's more than just a digital resume—it's a powerful platform to showcase your expertise, build credibility, and attract the right opportunities. Here's how to strategically boost your visibility and elevate your presence:

☑ Optimize Your LinkedIn Profile
Make a strong first impression with a profile that communicates who you are, what you do best, and where you're headed.

Craft a Targeted, Memorable Headline
Use one of these powerful formats to stand out in searches and immediately convey your value:
Format 1:
- **[Target Role or Function] | [Top Strength or Differentiator] | [Industry/Impact Focus]**
- Example: Marketing Strategist | Data-Driven Growth | SaaS & Tech

Format 2:
- I help **[Audience] [Achieve What]** by **[How You Do It]**
- Example: I help mission-driven teams scale impact by aligning strategy with execution.

Engaging About Section
Tell your professional story in a clear, confident voice. Use this space to highlight your top strengths, key wins, and the kind of work you're excited to do next. Consider weaving in a personal touch, whether it's a passion, value, or interest, to humanize your profile and build connection.

Relevant Skills & Endorsements
Curate your Skills section with terms aligned to your target roles. Use job descriptions as inspiration and focus on high-impact, industry-relevant skills to boost your visibility in recruiter searches.

PRO TIP: LinkedIn's algorithm favors active, up-to-date profiles. A small tweak every few weeks (updating your headline, adding a new skill, or sharing a recent win) can increase your visibility in recruiter searches. Staying active signals that you're engaged, evolving, and ready for new opportunities.

🔑 Six Quick Wins for Recruiter Visibility

Even if you don't apply through the platform, your LinkedIn profile is one of the first things a recruiter will see, whether they find you through a search, Google your name from a resume, or browse their ATS (Applicant Tracking System) for past applicants.

These six quick wins help ensure your profile shows up in searches and makes a strong impression:

- **Turn On "Open to Work"**: Enable this setting and choose "recruiters only" if you prefer privacy. This makes your profile searchable for relevant openings.
- **Optimize Your Summary:** Your About section should reflect both where you've been and where you're going. Emphasize your expertise, recent results, and the kinds of opportunities you're exploring.
- **Highlight Industry-Specific Skills:** Use language from job postings to update your Skills section. LinkedIn's algorithm rewards keyword alignment.
- **Post & Engage Regularly:** Consistency builds visibility, but intentionality builds credibility. Don't just like and scroll—share your learning journey, industry insights, or reflections that showcase your evolving skill set and voice.
- **Turn Milestones Into Moments:** Instead of simply clicking the "Add to Profile" button when you complete a certification, transform it into a story. Share why you pursued the course, one key takeaway, and how you plan to apply what you learned in your next role.
- **Start Genuine Conversations:** Celebrate others' milestones, comment thoughtfully, and ask meaningful questions. This kind of engagement builds authentic relationships and increases your discoverability in the right circles.

LinkedIn's algorithm favors authentic interaction over passive scrolling, and so do recruiters. Think of every comment or post as a small signal of who you are, what you value, and how you show up in your field.

PRO TIP: Recruiters often pull profiles from their ATS when new roles open. If you've applied before, staying active keeps your profile warm and more likely to resurface.

☑ Engage Strategically

Regular, thoughtful activity helps you stay top of mind with your network and appear in more recruiter feeds.

- Share Content: Post industry insights, lessons learned, or articles with your own commentary.
- Comment Meaningfully: Add thoughtful takeaways to posts by recruiters, thought leaders, or peers.
- Use Strategic Hashtags: Expand your reach with tags like #Leadership, #TechCareers, or #JobSearchTips.

AI Prompt: Content Ideas for LinkedIn

"Based on my experience in **[industry/role]** and my strengths in **[list]**, suggest three types of professional LinkedIn posts I can share to build credibility and engagement while job searching."

Proactive Networking

LinkedIn is built for connection. Use it to grow your network and uncover new possibilities.

- Personalized Invites: Always include a note when sending connection requests. Mention a shared interest, mutual connection, or recent post.
- Follow-Up Thoughtfully: When reaching out, explain how your background aligns with mutual interests or goals.
- Request Informational Interviews: Use LinkedIn to ask for brief conversations to gain insights or learn more about a company or role.

☑ Leverage Recommendations and Endorsements

Social proof builds trust and strengthens your professional brand.

- Request Specific Recommendations: Ask for endorsements that highlight particular projects or strengths aligned with your goals.
- Give Thoughtful Endorsements: Boost visibility and goodwill by endorsing others for skills you've seen them demonstrate.

PRO TIP: Google yourself! See what employers will see. If you find outdated or irrelevant content:
- Adjust privacy settings.
- Remove or update old posts.
- Publish new, professional content to push down older results.

Think of your digital footprint as part of your overall brand. Make sure it supports your current career goals.

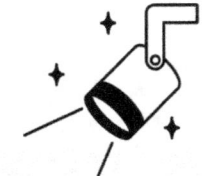

Visibility That Led to Interviews

After a corporate layoff from her mid-level marketing role, **Priya** realized her LinkedIn presence no longer reflected her strengths or goals. She took three focused actions:

Updated her headline to: "Growth-Focused Marketer | Campaign Optimization | Driving ROI in B2B Tech"

Posted an "Open to Work" update, tagging three target companies and sharing what she was excited to do next.

Prioritized daily comments on posts from marketing leaders and recruiters—adding value, not just likes.

The result? Within nine weeks, Priya's profile views more than doubled, and two hiring managers reached out directly through LinkedIn messaging to schedule interest calls.

Takeaway: Visibility isn't about going viral—it's about being findable. A relevant headline, thoughtful engagement, and intentional updates can make your profile a magnet for the right opportunities.

JOB SEEKER SPOTLIGHT

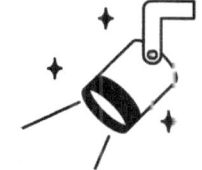

Building Credibility During a Career Pivot

Marcus wanted to transition from SaaS sales into sustainability consulting—a competitive, relationship-driven field. Instead of applying cold, he used LinkedIn to reposition himself:

Rewrote his About section to connect his sales achievements to purpose-driven business outcomes.

Reached out to alumni in sustainability and scheduled 15-minute insight calls.

Shared one article a week, adding brief reflections that linked sustainability trends to business performance.

Within ten weeks, Marcus had three informational interviews, two referrals, and a project-based consulting offer that aligned with his goals.

Takeaway: Position your profile for where you're headed, not just where you've been. Strategic storytelling and steady engagement can unlock new fields—even if you're just getting started.

Example: Post-Layoff Optimized LinkedIn Summary
Headline: Program Analyst | Process Optimization | Change Management | Open to Remote/Hybrid Roles | Based in Austin, TX

About: I'm a Program Analyst specializing in process optimization and change management, now ready to bring my expertise to the private sector after a recent federal workforce reduction.

Throughout my career, I've been the go-to person for breaking down silos, translating complex data into actionable insights, and leading change that drives measurable results. I thrive on uncovering hidden inefficiencies and building practical systems that stick.

Key Achievements:
☑ **Process Optimization:** Saved 15+ hours/week and boosted team efficiency by 20%, regaining 60+ hours/month across 4 departments.
☑ **Policy & Compliance**: Reduced regulatory risk by 35% with standardized frameworks, surpassing audit targets by 15%.
☑ **Stakeholder Engagement:** Led 12+ cross-functional teams to 98% initiative adoption, outperforming enterprise averages by 20%.
☑ **Data-Driven Strategy:** Delivered insights that shaped $2.3M in resource and policy decisions across 3 fiscal years.

Ideal Roles: Program Analyst | Operations Manager | Process Improvement Consultant | Change Management Specialist | Policy & Compliance Manager

Target Companies: I'm drawn to private sector, nonprofit, or consulting organizations that prioritize operational excellence and data-informed decision-making like #CareerPrompt, #[CompanyName], and # [CompanyName]. I'm especially interested in companies recognized for their commitment to innovation, measurable impact, and continuous improvement.

Key Skills: Process Improvement & Optimization | Change Management Strategy | Cross-Functional Collaboration | Data Analysis & Visualization | Compliance & Policy Design | Strategic Planning & Execution

If you're looking for someone who can uncover inefficiencies, lead strategic change, and deliver measurable outcomes, let's connect.

AI Toolkit: Upgrade Your LinkedIn Presence with Precision

You don't have to start from scratch or go it alone. Use the following AI prompts to strategically strengthen your LinkedIn profile, increase visibility with recruiters, and position yourself for the opportunities you want next. Grouped by outcome, these prompts help you fine-tune everything from your headline and summary to keyword optimization, visual branding, and connection-building. Simply copy, customize, and paste into your preferred AI tool to get started.

 AI Prompt: Full Profile Optimization

"Analyze my LinkedIn profile and suggest improvements to increase recruiter visibility, including a refined headline, About section, and keyword-optimized skills.
[Paste a copy/snapshot of your LinkedIn profile]"

"Optimize my LinkedIn headline to clearly highlight my expertise in **[specific role or industry]** to attract recruiter attention.
 Here are key details about my experience:
- Current/Past Job Titles: **[Insert]**
- Core Skills & Strengths: **[Insert]**
- Notable Achievements: **[Insert]**
- Industry Focus: **[Insert]**"

 **AI Prompt: Skills & Keyword Optimization**

"Analyze these job descriptions and generate a list of relevant industry keywords for my LinkedIn profile. Ensure the keywords are seamlessly incorporated into my About, Experience, and Skills sections for better recruiter visibility.
 [Paste example job descriptions + snapshot of your LinkedIn profile]"
"Identify the top 10 industry-relevant keywords missing from my current LinkedIn profile and suggest where to place them for maximum visibility."

AI Prompt: Strategic Summary

"Craft an optimized LinkedIn summary that highlights my skills **[list top skills]**, my professional experience in **[industry]**, and my openness to new opportunities. Ensure it includes industry-relevant keywords to improve recruiter search visibility. Here's key background information to include:

- Current Role & Expertise: **[Briefly summarize your key strengths]**
- Notable Career Achievements: **[List quantifiable results or impact]**
- What I'm Looking For Next: **[Specify your career goals]**"

 ### AI Prompt: Profile & Banner Photos

"Suggest visually appealing LinkedIn banner ideas that align with my industry **[your industry]** and reinforce my professional brand. The design should be clean, impactful, and recruiter-friendly."
[Paste a brief description of your brand]

 ### AI Prompt: Open To Work Post

"Generate a clear, concise, and compelling LinkedIn 'Open to Work' post showcasing my skills **[key skills]** and openness to roles in **[industry/field/location]**. Ensure it's professional yet engaging, and include ideal companies by name and tag them when possible to increase visibility."
[Paste a list of your ideal companies and why]

 ### AI Prompt: Recommendations & Endorsements

"Provide a concise yet friendly LinkedIn message template to request a recommendation from my former manager, highlighting my strengths in **[specific skill or project]**."

✎ **Reflection Prompt:**

What's one specific action you can take this week to elevate your LinkedIn presence and engage more meaningfully with your professional network?

ACTION STEP: Set aside 30 minutes to review and refresh your LinkedIn profile:
- Remove outdated information.
- Update your headline and summary.
- Add relevant keywords that align with your career goals and target roles.

Final Thoughts

LinkedIn isn't just a digital resume. It's your professional signal to the world. When you show up with clarity, consistency, and confidence, you attract attention and alignment. The right opportunities are out there. Make it easier for them to find you.

Clarify & Communicate
Your Career Brand

Your career brand uniquely combines your professional strengths, expertise, and personal values. It's what distinguishes you in a competitive job market and ensures you're remembered for the right reasons. Getting clear on your brand—and communicating it consistently—can significantly increase your visibility, credibility, and career opportunities.

☑ Define Your Professional Identity
Before others can recognize your value, you have to define it for yourself.
- **Identify Your Strengths:** Reflect on your top skills and strengths. Pull from past feedback, performance reviews, and projects where you made a clear difference.
- **Clarify Your Value:** What do you bring that others don't? What problems are you best at solving? What qualities make you someone people trust and want to work with?
- **Craft Your Brand Statement:** Create a concise, confident statement that communicates who you are, what you do best, and the impact you consistently deliver.

Example Brand Statements:
Public
- "I'm a marketing strategist who combines data-driven insight and narrative design to build campaigns that engage public audiences, support mission outcomes, and exceed program goals—especially in complex, multi-stakeholder environments."

Public Programs / Social Impact:
- "As a marketing strategist, I translate complex programs into accessible, audience-focused campaigns that drive engagement and exceed performance benchmarks—leveraging both creative storytelling and rigorous data analysis."

Hybrid (Public + Private):
- "I craft marketing strategies that merge data insight with compelling storytelling—building trust, driving measurable impact, and supporting both business and mission-focused goals across diverse sectors."

AI Prompt: Brand Statement Generator #1

"Based on my experience in **[insert industry or role]**, my top strengths are **[list 3–5]**, and I'm targeting roles in **[insert field or job title]**. Write a concise, confident career brand statement based on my resume (attached) that reflects my unique value, includes measurable impact or strengths where possible, and sounds natural when spoken or written."
[Upload your resume/Experience section]

 AI Prompt: Brand Statement Generator #2

"Write a career brand statement for a marketing strategist with experience in storytelling, data analytics, and campaign development. Focus on roles aligned with federal government or mission-driven organizations. Make it concise, concrete, and focused on measurable impact."

JOB SEEKER SPOTLIGHT

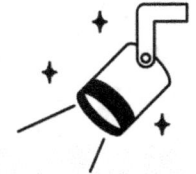

Aligning Brand to Break Through

After being laid off from a communications role, **Taylor** realized her resume blended in with countless others. She paused to reflect and uncovered her unique strength: translating complex messaging across global teams during high-stakes transitions.

She revamped her LinkedIn summary and began posting weekly insights on communication challenges in change management. Her content was specific, relevant, and backed by experience. Within three months, she was invited to speak on a podcast, and several of her posts were reshared by peers in the field, expanding her visibility.

One post caught the attention of a hiring manager in her target industry, who reached out directly.

Takeaway: When your brand is clearly defined and consistently shared, it does the heavy lifting for you. Clarity earns attention. Relevance opens doors.

✅ Align Your Communication

Your brand should show up wherever your career does—online, in documents, and in conversation.

- **LinkedIn & Online Profiles:** Make sure your headline, About section, and Skills reflect your brand's strengths and direction.
- **Resume & Cover Letters:** Infuse your brand language throughout your application materials. Make your differentiators obvious.
- **Networking Conversations:** Speak about your work with clarity and purpose. Your brand statement can guide elevator pitches intros, and responses.

Mini Brand Audit Checklist

Make sure your brand shows up consistently wherever your career shows up. Use this quick audit to assess whether your professional materials and interactions reflect your unique value and direction.

Clarity

☐ My brand statement clearly communicates what I do, how I do it, and the value I bring.

☐ I can articulate my top 3–5 strengths with confidence and specificity.

☐ I know what sets me apart from others in my field.

Consistency

☐ My LinkedIn headline and summary reflect my brand statement.

☐ My resume and cover letter use similar language, tone, and emphasis.

☐ I express the same core message in interviews and conversations.

Credibility

☐ I can demonstrate my brand through specific examples, metrics, or outcomes.

☐ My endorsements, testimonials, or recommendations reinforce my brand.

☐ I'm actively sharing or engaging with content that aligns with my brand.

Connection

☐ My brand reflects what I've done and where I'm going.

☐ My tone is authentic and human, not just polished or professional.

☐ I feel confident using this brand in conversations, online, and in person.

✅ Activate Your Brand Through Content

You don't have to post daily to build a strong personal brand. Thoughtful engagement and visible proof of your expertise go a long way. Think quality vs. quantity.

- **Showcase Credibility:** Share project wins, insights, client stories, or practical lessons. Highlight how you solve problems and deliver value.
- **Engage with Intention:** Comment on relevant posts with thoughtful takeaways. Repost with added context. Even brief reflections can position you as someone who thinks deeply and shows up with purpose.
- **Share Thought Leadership:** Focus on 3–5 signature themes. This helps people quickly understand what you're about—and remember you for it.
- **Start with Common Ground:** Unsure what to post? Think about the challenges your peers face, or offer perspective on trends in your field.

Reminder: You don't need to post every day to be visible, just intentionally. Thoughtful content every 1–2 weeks, paired with consistent, value-added comments, can keep you top-of-mind with the right people and reinforce your brand without burnout. Everyone has something worth sharing, especially you.

 AI Prompt: Content Ideas

"Suggest five LinkedIn post ideas for someone in **[your field]** looking to showcase expertise in **[signature theme]** and build a visible, authentic career brand."

JOB SEEKER SPOTLIGHT

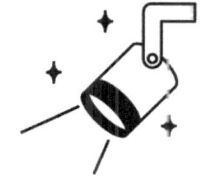

Using Strategic Vulnerability

Louis, a former DC-based product manager supporting public health tech solutions, struggled to explain his layoff. After reflecting on his experience, he decided to share a LinkedIn post about lessons learned from a complex pilot project that didn't reach its adoption targets, but still generated valuable user feedback that shaped future government contracts.

Instead of glossing over the challenges, Louis leaned into what the project revealed about resilience, user-centered design, and iterative problem-solving. His post gained traction on LinkedIn, especially among peers in health and human services tech. A hiring manager commented directly and later invited him to apply for a role focused on improving public service delivery through human-centered design.

Takeaway: Strategic vulnerability, when grounded in insight and learning, can boost credibility and connection. Sharing thoughtful reflections, even from imperfect outcomes, signals maturity, alignment, and mission-driven focus.

PRO TIP: Vulnerability isn't just about being open. It's about being intentional. The most memorable posts connect a personal story with a professional insight. Show what you've learned and why it matters.

✎ **Reflection Prompt:**

What 3–5 topics would I want to be known for in my industry or field? What am I often asked about or passionate about sharing?

 AI Prompt: Build Your Brand Content Themes

"Based on my experience in **[field]** and the **[roles I'm targeting]**, suggest 3–5 content topics or themes that reflect my expertise and career brand. I want to build credibility, not just visibility."

Before submitting this prompt, be sure to copy and paste your resume (or upload it, if using a platform that allows file input). Doing so gives the AI the context it needs to tailor the content themes to your unique experience and goals.

Final Thoughts

Your brand is what you do, how you do it, and why it matters. When you define your value and communicate it with conficence, you shift from job seeker to opportunity magnet. You don't need to be braggadocious—just real. Let your story reflect where you're headed, not just where you've been.

Interviewing: Communicate Value & Personality

Interviewing post-layoff is an opportunity to demonstrate resilience, clarity, and professionalism. Below is a strategic approach to addressing your layoff while showcasing your unique strengths and personality.

☑ Reframe Your Layoff Experience
Strategically position your layoff as a catalyst for growth:
- Concise Explanation: "Due to company-wide restructuring, my department was downsized. While unexpected, it's given me clarity about where I want to contribute next."
- Highlight Growth: "I've deepened my project management skills during this transition and completed a certification in agile methodologies."
- Show Personality: "I'm someone who thrives in collaborative environments where creative problem-solving matters—which is why I'm excited about this role."

☑ Master the ROAR Method
Transform scripted answers into compelling stories that showcase how you think, lead, and make an impact by using the ROAR framework—Results, Objective, Action, and Reinforced Results.

- Result (Lead with impact): Clearly state the positive outcome you achieved.
- Objective: Briefly describe your goal or the problem you needed to solve.
- Action: Outline specific steps you took to achieve the result.
- Reinforced Results: Reaffirm and emphasize how your actions directly led to achieving the impactful result.

Example Question:
"Can you share an accomplishment you're particularly proud of?"

ROAR Response:

"Early in my career, I discovered a passion for solving operational puzzles. One challenge stands out: our team was overwhelmed by overtime costs tied to inefficient project timelines (Objective). Determined to find a better way, I researched solutions, championed a new project management tool, and led agile training sessions—often staying late to create easy-to-use reference guides (Action).

The results were immediate. We reduced project completion time by 20% and saved thousands in overtime expenses (Result). But what I'm most proud of? We sparked a culture shift. Teammates began sharing ideas and leading improvements. To this day, some still joke that I "infected" them with agile thinking (Reinforced Results)."

 AI Prompt: Scripted to Storytelling (ROAR Method)

"Here's my ROAR response: **[Insert]**. Make it sound like I'm telling a story to a colleague over coffee. Include a brief personal detail (e.g., why this mattered to me) and emphasize how my unique approach solved the problem. Ensure it flows smoothly, avoids repetitive sentence patterns, and feels like a compelling story rather than a script."
You can also ask AI to shorten or expand your response as needed.

☑ **Prepare & Practice Strategically**
Balance polish with authenticity. Common Questions:
- "Tell me about yourself" → "I'm a data-driven strategist who geeked out over process optimization long before it was trendy—here's how that passion shaped my career..."
- "Why leave your last role?" → "The layoff clarified my desire to work in environments that prioritize [specific value aligned with company]."
- Practice Aloud: Silent prep can feel productive, but it rarely sticks. Instead, record yourself answering key questions, then listen back as you would your favorite playlist. In the first few rounds, notice where you sound stiff, robotic, or unsure. As you keep listening, you'll catch your natural rhythm and enthusiasm. This repetition helps you internalize your message, respond more fluidly, and confidently showcase your strengths in real conversations.
- Body Language: Smile when discussing achievements. Lean slightly forward when emphasizing key points.

Interview Voice Toolkit

Your tone, pace, and presence matter just as much as your words.

Inspired by speaker and communication coach Vinh Giang, these delivery tools can elevate even your best stories:

🗣 Use Vocal Variety
Even strong answers fall flat in a monotone. Match your pacing and pitch to the emotional beats of your story.

Voice Tool	Try This	Personality Tip
Pitch	Lower slightly for serious points; rise when sharing enthusiasm	*"This project lit me up because..."*
Pace	Slow for key results; quicken when describing action	*"We moved FAST—but here's how we kept quality high."*
Volume	Increase slightly when stating values or achievements	*"I'm particularly proud of..."*
Pauses	1-2 second pause before/after important points	*"We reduced processing time by 40%... (pause) and rolled out the new workflow across four departments."*

 Best Practices for Virtual Interviews

Even when you're remote, how you show up still speaks volumes. Most first-round interviews are still virtual, so make the most of the medium with these small but powerful moves:

☑ Show personality through the screen
- Lighting: Use natural light or a ring light to ensure your expressions are visible, and position your camera at eye level.
- Background: Include one subtle personal item (plant, artwork) to feel grounded. Keep it simple and distraction-free. Sit centered in the frame and make sure your face and torso are visible—not too close, not too far.
- Energy: Imagine you're explaining ideas to a curious friend, not performing.

- Tech Check: Test for "Can you hear my dog's collar jingle?" moments beforehand.
- Look into the camera—not the screen—when speaking. It creates the feeling of direct eye contact and builds connection, even virtually.

☑ Dress for the Role
- Wear what you would to an in-person interview, even if it's a video call. It boosts confidence and shows respect for the process.

☑ Minimize Interruptions
- Silence notifications, close browser tabs, and let anyone you live with know you'll need quiet time.

☑ Own the Conversation

Start strong with personality-infused statements:
- "I've been described as a 'bridge-builder' between teams—let me share how that played out in my last role."
- "You'll find I'm equal parts analytical and creative—here's an example..."
- "I'm at my best when **[specific work scenario that aligns with role]**."

PRO TIPS:
- For virtual interviews, position a small photo of a supportive person near your camera to naturally soften your expression. Keep a printed copy of your resume and key notes nearby, but don't read from them. Speak from preparation, not a script.
- End with a memorable, value-driven question:
  - "What's one challenge your team is facing that someone with my **[specific skill/passion]** could help solve?"

✍ **Reflection Prompt**
- What energy do I want to bring into this room?
- What does my tone, pace, or posture say about me—before I even finish my first sentence?

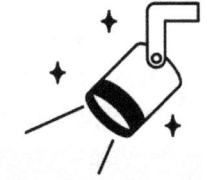

Turning Disappointment into Confidence

After being laid off from her HR Business Partner role due to a company-wide restructure, not performance, **Jenny** jumped into interviews immediately. But she quickly hit a roadblock: explaining her layoff while still demonstrating value. Her early interviews felt defensive and overly scripted.

Instead of giving up, she hit pause. Jenny began practicing with the ROAR method to craft clear, impact-driven stories. She recorded herself to refine her tone, simplify her language, and sound more like herself. She also took time to reflect on what didn't go well, and used each interview as a feedback loop.

By her third interview, everything shifted. When asked about her layoff, she briefly acknowledged the restructure, then confidently pivoted to a story that showed her impact:

*"The restructure clarified my passion for employee experience. For example, I led a well-being initiative that reduced turnover by 18% **(Result)**. We were seeing burnout in hybrid teams **(Objective)**, so I partnered with IT to launch pulse surveys and rolled out manager training **(Action)**. Now, I help leaders see retention as a leading indicator, not just an HR metric **(Reinforced Result)**."*

She advanced to the final round and was told her self-awareness and clarity made her stand out.

Takeaway: Your first interviews may be rough, which is normal. Jenny turned early missteps into momentum by learning, practicing, and showing up with intention.

PRO TIPS: Take advantage of free interview practice tools like:

- Google Interview Warmup - Created by Google as part of their Career Certificates program.
- Pramp - Established platform with a solid reputation in the tech industry.
- Big Interview - Developed by career experts and used by many universities and career centers.
- LinkedIn Interview Preparation - Official tool from LinkedIn, a trusted professional networking platform
- Indeed Interview Practice - Offered by Indeed, one of the world's largest job sites.
- InterviewBit - Well-regarded in the tech community for technical interview preparation.
- Jobscan Interview - From the same company that provides the widely used resume optimization tool.

These platforms offer realistic question scenarios, peer-to-peer practice, and valuable feedback that can significantly boost your interview confidence and performance without any financial investment.

☑ Effective Follow-Up

Professional follow-up reinforces your interest and leaves a lasting impression.

- Prompt & Polite: Send a personalized thank-you email within 24 hours.
- Reaffirm Interest: Briefly reiterate your interest in the role and highlight a specific part of your conversation that resonated with you.
- Address Remaining Questions, If Needed: Use this opportunity to tactfully clarify any unclear answers or share additional insights relevant to the role.

PRO TIPS:

- Connecting with employees before your interview can give you valuable insight and a potential internal advocate. On LinkedIn, search "**[Company Name]** + People" and filter by department or job title to find relevant contacts. A short, thoughtful message can go a long way.
- Interview prep matters, but authenticity matters more. Instead of memorizing answers word-for-word, focus on internalizing key stories, examples, and takeaways. This helps your responses sound natural, confident, and human, especially when addressing sensitive topics like layoffs.

✍ **Reflection Prompt:**

How can I share the story of my layoff with clarity and confidence, while highlighting the growth, insight, and professional value I'm bringing into my next opportunity?

Turning Job Descriptions into Interview Questions

AI can be a powerful practice partner. One smart prompt can convert a job description into tailored interview questions and help you refine your responses using the ROAR framework.

 AI Prompt: Mock Interview Simulator with Feedback

"Act as a hiring manager conducting an interview for a **[Job Title]** role in the **[Industry]** field. Ask me 5 behavioral interview questions based on this job description: **[Paste Job Description]**. After I answer each question, evaluate my response using the ROAR framework. Highlight what I did well, what could be improved, and how to make it more concise, impactful, or confident. Keep the tone supportive and focused on growth."

How This Helps:

☑ Saves time by automatically converting job requirements into likely interview questions.

☑ Ensures alignment between your responses and what employers are actually looking for.

☑ Strengthens answers by reinforcing achievement-driven storytelling through the ROAR framework.

ACTION STEP: Choose a job description you're targeting and run it through the AI mock interview prompt. Respond using the ROAR method. Then, review the AI's feedback and identify one improvement per answer—whether to make it more concise, clearer, or more compelling. Repeat weekly to build confidence and fluency.

✅ Navigate Tough Questions with Confidence

When Discussing a Layoff:

- Keep it brief and neutral (e.g., "due to a company-wide restructure.")
- Shift focus to what you've gained—skills, insight, momentum.
- Pivot to a strong ROAR story that reinforces your value.

✅ **When Asked About Salary:** Avoid giving a number too early. Instead, try:

"I'd be happy to discuss compensation once I have a full understanding of the role's scope. In the meantime, could you share the salary range budgeted for this position?"

✅ Own Your Worth at the Offer Stage

Many candidates hesitate when money comes up, but salary conversations don't have to feel intimidating, especially when you're prepared with both market data and a clear understanding of your own value.

- Pair Market Ranges with Value-Based Framing: Salary tools like Glassdoor, Levels.fyi, Salary.com, and LinkedIn Salary Insights can offer a helpful starting point, but ranges are often broad. Go deeper by connecting your compensation expectations to the value you bring:
  - Your track record of delivering results
  - Specialized skills or certifications
  - Industry demand for your role
  - Unique differentiators (e.g., bilingual skills, turnaround expertise, leadership experience)
- Practice Your Ask: *"Based on what I've achieved, the market range I've researched, and the value I bring, I'm targeting a compensation package in the range of [$X–$Y]. Is that aligned with your budget for this role?"*
- Be Ready for Counteroffers: If the offer is lower than expected, respond with:

"Thanks for the offer. Based on my skills and the results I've consistently delivered, I was expecting something closer to [$X]. Is there room to bridge the gap?"

When They Share a Range: Try This

"Thanks for sharing the range. Given my experience in **[area]** and past results like **[insert brief example]**, I'd be aiming for the higher end. I'm open to discussing the full package, including benefits."

"Appreciate the transparency. With **[X]** years of experience in **[relevant skill]** and a track record of **[brief result]**, I'd love to discuss how that aligns with your compensation framework or step level."

 ## When the Range Is Fixed (Federal/Public Sector)

"Thanks for walking me through the range. Given my **[number]** years of relevant experience, especially in **[insert related area]**, and my track record in **[quick win or achievement]**, I'd be interested in discussing how that might inform the starting step or grade level. I'm also open to understanding the full package, including benefits or other incentives."

> **PRO TIP:** Rather than focusing solely on a salary figure, be ready to speak to the full package: performance bonuses, equity, development support, wellness benefits, flexibility, and advancement potential. When you frame compensation as part of a bigger value exchange, you shift the conversation from cost to contribution.

 ### Final Thoughts

Interviewing is about what you say and how you show up. The most powerful thing you can bring into the room is your ability to share a clear, compelling story of who you are, how you've grown, the impact you've made, and where you're headed next.

Remember: interviews are a two-way street. Employers are evaluating you, but you're also gathering the information you need to make an informed decision if an offer comes. Asking thoughtful questions, assessing alignment, and observing culture in real time helps ensure better outcomes for both sides.

Networking With Confidence

Successful networking today isn't about small talk or transactional asks. It's about building real relationships rooted in trust, relevance, and mutual value. Whether you're job searching, pivoting industries, or nurturing long-term career growth, intentional connection is your edge.

☑ Approach Networking with a Strategic Mindset
Networking that drives momentum is focused, not scattered.
- **Clarify Your Why:** Are you looking for insight, visibility, mentorship, referrals, or collaboration? Knowing your purpose helps shape more intentional conversations.
- **Prioritize Alignment:** Focus on connecting with individuals whose work, mission, or career path aligns with where you're headed, not just where you've been.
- **Lead with Value:** Offer before you ask. Share relevant insights, amplify their work, or connect them with someone in your network. Generosity builds trust.

Reminder: Networking is about planting seeds for future opportunity, credibility, and community.

☑ Master the Art of Reconnecting
Rekindle existing connections with warmth and purpose.
- **Reach Out at Natural Moments:** Congratulate them on a promotion, new role, or post you found valuable. Timeliness keeps it organic.
- **Be Direct and Considerate:** Briefly mention why you're reaching out and how reconnecting could benefit both of you.
- **Make the Next Step Easy**: Suggest a short call, virtual coffee chat, or async voice memo exchange—whatever feels low-pressure but forward-moving.

Sample Message:
"Hi **[Name]**, I saw your recent post about **[topic]** and it really resonated. I'd love to reconnect and hear more about your work in **[field]**. Would you be open to a quick 15-minute chat sometime this month?"

✅ Maximize Informational Interviews

Informational interviews are powerful for career insight and access, especially when tapping into weak ties, not just close contacts.

- **Target Wisely:** Reach out to people whose career paths you admire, especially those one or two steps ahead of you in roles, industries, or pivots.
- **Ask Smarter Questions:** Skip "what do you do?" and dig deeper:
  - "What trends are shaping your team's priorities right now?"
  - "What's one shift you made that really leveled up your career?"
  - "Looking back, what would you have done sooner in your transition?"
- **Stay Connected:** Send a thank-you message, share how their advice helped, or follow up with an article or update they'd appreciate. Relationships are built through consistency, not just one conversation.

 ### What's a Weak Tie (and Why It Matters)?

A weak tie is someone you know lightly—a former colleague, a conference connection, a LinkedIn acquaintance. They're one of your most underutilized resources.

Research shows that weak ties often open doors to new roles, industries, and introductions because they extend beyond your existing circles.
✅ Strong ties = trust and comfort
✅ Weak ties = reach and opportunity

Don't underestimate the power of a warm, well-timed check-in. One thoughtful message can create new possibilities.

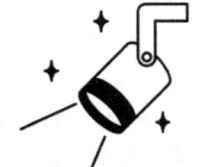

Unlocking Opportunity Through Weak Ties

After being laid off from her mid-level role at a federal agency, **Nia** was ready for a new chapter, but she faced a challenge: her experience and network were almost entirely government-facing, and she wanted to pivot into the private sector.

Instead of mass applying to roles online, Nia paused to reflect on her existing connections. She remembered a cross-sector collaboration from a few years back and reached out to a policy consultant she'd only spoken to a few times. Her message was simple: *"I'm navigating a career pivot and curious about your path. Would you be open to a brief conversation?"*

That 15-minute chat led to two warm introductions—one of which turned into an informational interview at a tech-enabled social impact firm. She stayed in touch with the team, shared insights on government partnerships, and four months later, landed a strategy role focused on public-private innovation.

Takeaway: Your next opportunity may come from someone you haven't spoken to in years, or only met once. In today's market, weak ties often become strong bridges when you lead with curiosity, value, and earnestness about your direction.

✅ Leverage Your Network Strategically

In today's job market, where referrals often outpace job boards, building intentional relationships is your secret advantage. Strategic networking is about expanding your contact list and creating ongoing, value-based dialogue with the right people.

- **Map Your Connectors:** Identify people in your network with cross-industry visibility, trusted influence, or experience in your desired field. These "connectors" are often the bridge to roles and insights you won't find publicly posted.
- **Offer Value First:** Share something useful before making an ask. It could be a timely article, an industry trend, a job lead for someone else, or a podcast related to their current work. Tailored, relevant engagement leaves a lasting impression.
- **Keep Reciprocity Alive:** Stay on the radar by checking in, celebrating their wins, and offering support. Helping others reinforces your reputation as someone worth knowing and referring.

Sample Outreach Message:
*"Hi, **[Name],** I hope you're doing well! I'm currently exploring new opportunities in **[industry or role]**, and given your experience and network, I thought of you. If anything comes to mind—whether it's an opening, someone I should connect with, or general insight—I'd be so grateful. Either way, I'd love to catch up briefly if you're open!"*

✎ Reflection Prompt:

Who could you reach out to this week, and what thoughtful gesture, resource, or insight could you share to nurture the connection?

AI Prompt: Draft a Thoughtful Connection Request

"Write a brief, professional LinkedIn connection request to someone in **[target role/industry]**, referencing a recent article or project of theirs. Keep the tone warm, authentic, and purposeful."

PRO TIPS:
- **The Fastest Path to a Job?** It's Not Applying. Around **70%** of jobs are filled through networking, not through applications alone. The more tailored and intentional your outreach, the better your odds.
- Lead with **Curiosity**, Not Desperation. Ask thoughtful, open-ended questions like:
  - "What's been the most exciting shift in your work lately?"
  - "What's something you wish more people understood about your industry right now?"

This positions you as a peer, not just a job seeker.

Reframing Your Layoff in Networking Conversations

When you're networking, especially informally or through mutual contacts, you don't owe anyone a deep dive into why your last role ended. The purpose of these conversations is to build connection, not defend your resume. Here are simple, confident ways to frame it:

Confident, Modern Scripts

Concise & Neutral:
"Due to a company-wide restructure, my position was eliminated. I'm now exploring roles where I can apply my skills in [key strength or focus area]."

Growth-Oriented:
"My last role ended due to organizational changes. I'm using this transition as a chance to pivot into opportunities that align with my passion for [industry challenge or strength], especially in [desired type of environment or team.]"

Future-Focused:
"After a recent layoff, I'm excited to find a role where I can bring my skills in [insert] to support teams focused on [goal or impact.]"

Exploratory & Open-Ended:
"My role was impacted by recent shifts in the organization. I'm in a season of exploring what's next and would really value your insights on [industry trends, emerging roles, or shifts you're seeing.]"

Layoffs are common and no longer carry the stigma they once did. especially in today's shifting economy. What stands out is how you show up in the conversation: self-aware, resourceful, and focused on the future.

PRO TIPS:
- **Skip the long story:** You don't need to relive the layoff. Keep it brief, grounded, and centered on what's next.
- **Own the narrative:** A calm, clear explanation signals emotional intelligence and resilience.
- **Bridge to value:** Transition quickly to your strengths, interests, or the kind of opportunities you're excited to explore.

ACTION STEPS: Build Connection, Not Just Contacts

☐Identify 5 organizations of interest: Choose companies, agencies, or mission-driven orgs that align with your values, skillset, or curiosity, not just your past titles.

☐Find 2 strategic contacts at each: Target alumni, peers in adjacent roles, hiring managers, or team leads. Look for people who reflect where you're headed, not just where you've been.

☐Send 5 thoughtful messages this week: Make your outreach human, low-pressure, and purposeful. Reference a post, project, or shared interest to personalize your message. (Use the sample scripts or AI prompts if needed.)

☐Schedule 2 informational chats in the next 2 weeks: Approach these as collaborative learning exchanges—not interviews. Come prepared with a few open-ended questions like:
- "What trends or shifts are you noticing in your team or industry right now that someone breaking in should be aware of?"
- "If you were making a career move today, what criteria would matter most to you in choosing your next opportunity?"

☐Track and reflect: After each conversation, jot down insights, potential follow-ups, and what gave you energy or clarity. Send a genuine thank-you, and stay in touch.

Smart Messaging for Recruiter Outreach

Initial Contact (DM or Email):
Hi, **[Recruiter's Name]**, I came across your work in **[specific industry or hiring area]**, and I'm currently exploring new opportunities that align with my background in **[your skill/role]**. I'd love to connect and learn if any current or upcoming roles might be a good fit. Either way, I appreciate the chance to stay in touch.

Follow-Up Message (Post-Chat):
Hi, **[Recruiter's Name]**, thanks again for the insightful conversation on **[topic or trend]**. I really valued your perspective. If any roles ar se that align with my experience in **[brief focus]**, I'd be glad to reconnect. Let's keep the lines open; I'll be following your work closely.

✍ **Reflection Prompt:**
What connection or conversation challenged your thinking or gave you unexpected clarity? How might you keep that dialogue alive in a way that's meaningful for both of you?

 AI Prompt: Thoughtful Follow-Up Message

"Write a warm, authentic follow-up message to someone I had an informational interview with. I'll include one takeaway from the conversation. Please incorporate it naturally, express appreciation, and keep the tone curious yet professional. Leave the door open for future connection or collaboration."
[Insert your takeaway.]

Final Thoughts

Networking after a layoff is less about pitching and more about positioning. You're reconnecting and realigning with purpose, and cultivating relationships based on mutual value.

The most effective connections happen because you lead with intention, generosity, and curiosity.

Negotiation Essentials:
Secure the Best Offer

Negotiation isn't just about getting more, but getting what's aligned, beyond salary. After a layoff, it's natural to feel urgency, but that doesn't mean you should settle. This stage is your opportunity to shape your next role around your goals, values, and worth.

☑ **Reframe Your Mindset**
Negotiation is expected, not awkward or a confrontation. Employers anticipate it, and when done respectfully, it reflects preparation and professionalism.
- **Detach Worth from the Layoff:** You're not negotiating your past. You're negotiating the value you're bringing forward. Your layoff doesn't define your leverage; your skills, results, and fit do.
- **Know the Market—and the Moment:** Use sites like Glassdoor, Levels.fy , Payscale, or Compa to benchmark competitive compensation for your role, industry, and region. Factor in post-layoff hiring trends and talent market shifts.

☑ **Anticipate Early Conversations**
Negotiation starts before the offer, often as early as the first conversation. Practice clarity and confidence when salary or expectations come up.

When asked for salary expectations:
"I'm happy to discuss compensation once we've explored mutual fit. That said, based on my research, experience, impact in similar work, I'd expect something in the range of [X–Y]."

When you receive an offer:
"Thank you for the offer. I'm excited about the opportunity. I'd like a couple of days to review the details and reflect. Can I get back to you by [insert weekday that's 2 days from initial offer]?"

☑ Go Beyond Base Salary

A strong offer includes both compensation and quality of life. Here are other areas you may be able to negotiate, especially in today's flexible, value-conscious job market:

- Signing bonus/equity (i.e., shares in the company, if applicable)
- Certification reimbursement or tuition assistance
- Professional development funds
- Remote/hybrid work flexibility (work-life harmony)
- Additional PTO or floating holidays
- Paid caregiver or family leave
- Wellness stipends or daycare reimbursement
- Retirement contributions or 401(k) matching
- Job title or role scope
- Performance-based bonuses

Sample Counteroffer Script:

*"Thank you again for the offer. Based on the scope of the role and market benchmarks, I'd like to propose a base salary of **[$X]**. I also noticed the offer includes **[X]** days of PTO annually—my preference would be **[Y]** days, to support work-life balance. I'm confident I can contribute immediate value in **[insert area]**, and I'd love to co-create an offer that feels mutually aligned."*

Common Pitfalls to Avoid

✗ Accepting an offer on the spot. Always ask for time to review.
✗ Focusing only on salary and overlooking benefits and flexibility.
✗ Leading with personal needs instead of professional value.

JOB SEEKER SPOTLIGHT

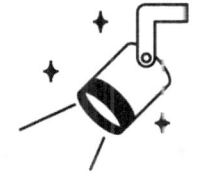

Negotiating Beyond the Salary Bump

After being laid off from his federal policy role, **Jonah**, a seasoned analyst and father of two, found himself with a tough but promising decision: two offers on the table. One came with a higher base salary. The other? Slightly less pay, but a clear path for advancement, mentorship from respected leaders, and a culture rooted in flexibility and continuous learning.

With rising childcare and healthcare costs top of mind, the bigger paycheck was tempting. But Jonah paused to ask a deeper question: *"Which role supports the life I'm building—not just the bills I'm paying?"*

He chose the second offer and negotiated intentionally. Instead of trying to match the higher salary, Jonah focused on what mattered most:
- ☑ Funding for certifications
- ☑ Flexible remote options
- ☑ Clear support for career development

His negotiation wasn't adversarial; it was collaborative. He positioned his asks around how they would help him show up fully, grow faster, and add more value to the organization long-term.

Takeaway: The best offer isn't always the biggest paycheck. Sometimes the smartest move is designing a role that aligns with your life, learning, and long-term goals, not just your income today.

JOB SEEKER SPOTLIGHT

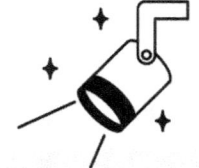

From Underselling to Advocating with Confidence

When **Marisol** was laid off from her public sector role in Sacramento, she was battling self-doubt. After years in government, she worried private sector employers might see her as too "institutional," or question her ability to thrive in fast-paced, innovation-driven environments.

But instead of playing small, Marisol leaned into strategy.
☑ She benchmarked compensation using current market data.
☑ She reconnected with colleagues who had successfully transitioned.
☑ She worked with a coach to clarify her value and practiced how to communicate it confidently.

When the offer came, she didn't settle. Marisol negotiated:
- A 12% increase in base salary
- Flexible remote work options
- A professional development budget to support continuous growth

She didn't overexplain her layoff. She led with evidence: quantifiable wins in cross-agency collaboration and streamlined operations. The hiring manager later shared that her presence during the negotiation signaled leadership before she even started the role.

Takeaway: Confidence doesn't come from having all the answers. It comes from knowing your worth and communicating it with intention. Employers who see your value will meet you at that level.

PRO TIPS:
- **Speak it to own it:** Rehearse your ask out loud, more than once. Confidence is built in the body as much as the brain. When your language feels familiar, it sounds natural and lands stronger.
- **Lead with value, not just data:** Market benchmarks give you a baseline. But your impact is what differentiates you. Anchor your ask in how you solve problems, drive results, or bring unique insight to the table.
- **Context is currency:** Compensation is fluid. Cost of living, remote work expectations, and shifts in high-demand roles all influence fair pay. Don't rely on last year's numbers—stay updated, and advocate accordingly.

AI Prompts for Confident Negotiation Prep

Use these to sharpen your language, clarify your range, and get comfortable leading the conversation.

To Start the Conversation (Pre-offer)

"Write a confident but flexible response to a salary expectations question. I want to express openness, highlight my value, and postpone specifics until I understand the full role scope."

To Benchmark and Articulate Value

"Help me craft a concise negotiation message that references market data, highlights my impact in **[specific skill or result]**, and respectfully requests a salary in the **[$X–$Y]** range."

For Tougher Moments in Negotiation

 To Handle Pushback or Low Offers

"Write a calm, confident message in response to a salary offer that's lower than expected. Help me express appreciation, reaffirm my value and alignment, and ask if there's room to revisit the offer, without sounding defensive."

 To Practice Under Pressure

"Act as a hiring manager and simulate a salary negotiation with me. Ask typical employer questions, push back on compensation requests, and coach me on how to respond assertively, and respectfully."

✎ **Reflection Prompt:**

Am I evaluating this offer through alignment or urgency?

What elements of this (or any) offer support my long-term career satisfaction, personal well-being, and professional growth?

- Does this role move me toward my bigger goals, or just away from discomfort?
- Am I compromising on something essential, or making a strategic trade-off?
- What would make this offer feel sustainable, not just acceptable?

Negotiation Essentials Checklist

Your clear, confidence-building guide to prepare, evaluate, and negotiate offers that align with your value and your life.

✅ **BEFORE THE INTERVIEW: Lay the Groundwork**

☐ **Define Your Ideal Range:** Clarify both your target and your *walkaway* number, grounded in current benchmarks, your financial needs, and the unique value you offer.

☐ **Research Compensation Trends:** Use platforms like Payscale, Levels.fyi, Glassdoor, Compa, or even LinkedIn Salary Insights. Prioritize data by industry, geography, and seniority level.

☐ **Identify Your Non-Negotiables:** Flag 2–3 high-impact benefits beyond base pay (e.g., remote flexibility, growth stipends, wellness perks, schedule autonomy).

☐ **Craft a Value Anchor Statement:** Write a summary of your core strengths and measurable results—this becomes your north star for negotiation.

☐ **Practice Out Loud:** Use mock interviews, AI role-play, or a trusted peer to rehearse how you'll articulate your ask with composure and confidence.

✅ **AFTER YOU RECEIVE AN OFFER: Evaluate Strategically**

☐ **Review the Entire Compensation Package:** Look at everything: salary, healthcare, retirement, equity, PTO, bonuses, title, and role scope.

☐ **Compare Against Your Needs + Market Trends:** Factor in cost of living, inflation, and any financial changes post-layoff.

☐ **Create a Comparison Matrix:** Score the offer based on alignment with your values, career growth, lifestyle needs, and earning potential.

☐ **List 1–2 Negotiation Priorities:** What matters most? Salary? Flexibility? Title? Pick your lead asks and be ready to support them with value-based reasoning.

☐ **Always Request the Offer in Writing:** Verbal offers are not official. Ask for the details in writing before making a final decision.

✅ **DURING THE NEGOTIATION: Lead With Clarity**

☐ **Ask About the Range:** If the employer hasn't shared it, ask directly and professionally: *"Can you share the budgeted range for this role?"*

☐ Lead with Value, Then Make the Ask. Use this structure:
*"Based on my experience driving **[impact]**, I'd love to explore a package closer to **[$X]**, aligned with the scope of this role."*

☐ Don't Over-Explain—Pause: State your ask, then stop. Silence after your proposal gives space for a response and shows confidence.

□ **Have a Backup Plan:** Prepare thoughtful, non-combative responses for lowball offers: *"Would it be possible to revisit this once I've had the chance to demonstrate my impact?"*

□ **Keep the Door Open:** *"I'm genuinely excited about this role and want to find a solution that reflects both the value I bring and the organization's goals."*

PRO TIP: You don't have to negotiate everything. Know the top 1–2 elements that would make this offer sustainable and satisfying, and lead with those.

Final Thoughts

Negotiation is a strategy, not a showdown; one grounded in preparation, clarity, and self-respect. You're shaping the conditions that will influence your time, energy, financial future, and long-term growth.

Especially after a layoff, it's easy to default to urgency. But slowing down, even slightly, to ask the right questions can reshape your entire trajectory. You've rebuilt. Now it's time to own your next chapter, on your terms.

Handling No's
and Moving Forward

Rejection is an inevitable part of any job search, but that doesn't make it feel any easier. Even the most qualified, well-prepared candidates hear "no" more than once. What matters most isn't the no itself but how you respond, reflect, and regroup. When handled objectively, rejection can sharpen your strategy, strengthen your narrative, and ultimately lead you closer to an opportunity that genuinely fits.

Before we talk about how to bounce back, let's name something important:

● Let's Talk About Bias in the Hiring Process

Here's a truth that doesn't get acknowledged enough: Even when you prepare thoroughly, present your best self, and check every box, rejection can still happen. And it's not always a reflection of your qualifications, your potential, or your effort.

Hiring decisions are made by humans. And humans bring bias, both implicit and explicit, into every step of the process. From assumptions about names, schools, work gaps, age, race, gender, neurodiversity, and more, bias plays a role in shaping how your materials are reviewed, how your responses are interpreted, and how you're evaluated after just one or two brief conversations.

But it's not just about identity or background. Sometimes the hiring outcome is shaped by something as small as the kind of day the interviewer is having. Stress, burnout, or distractions can influence how your answers land, or whether they're heard clearly at all. Even subtle things like the font on your resume, the domain of your email address (e.g., Yahoo vs. Gmail), or your style of communication can spark unconscious reactions. In a process that often moves quickly, snap judgments are made based on limited context, and they don't always reflect the full story of who you are or what you bring.

This isn't a reason to become paranoid, but it is a reason to stay grounded in self-awareness and self-compassion. Some hiring decisions, life-changing as they may be, are made by someone who interacted with you for an hour or less. That's the reality. And it's why rejection should never be taken as a definitive statement about your worth.

So yes, refine your story. Polish your materials. Practice your presence. But also remember: You are navigating a system that's imperfect, human, and sometimes unfair. Do your best, and let go of what you were never meant to control.

Now that we've acknowledged the human (and sometimes unfair) elements of hiring, let's explore how to reframe rejection in ways that serve your growth, not your doubt.

Reframing Rejection: It's About Fit, Not Failure

✅ **Zoom Out and Contextualize:** Hiring decisions are influenced by many variables—some of which you'll never see:

- Internal candidates
- Budget cuts
- Timing mismatches
- Team dynamics or culture shifts

A rejection is not a verdict on your value; it's a reflection of fit in that moment.

✅ **Protect Your Self-Worth:** You are not your resume. Your worth doesn't decrease with a rejection. Detach your identity from the outcome and focus on progress, not perfection.

✅ **Turn Setbacks Into Strategy:** Each "no" holds data. Were your responses specific enough? Did your application align with the job's actual needs? Were your salary expectations misaligned? Use rejection as a feedback loop to refine your process.

✅ **Evaluate Patterns with Curiosity:** If you're:

- Getting interviews but not progressing → Revisit your storytelling and clarity on the value you bring.
- Consistently not making it past initial screens → Audit resume alignment, salary range, or keyword usage.
- Losing energy or direction → Reassess the roles or industries you're targeting.

Rejection is rarely personal. But it can be directional.

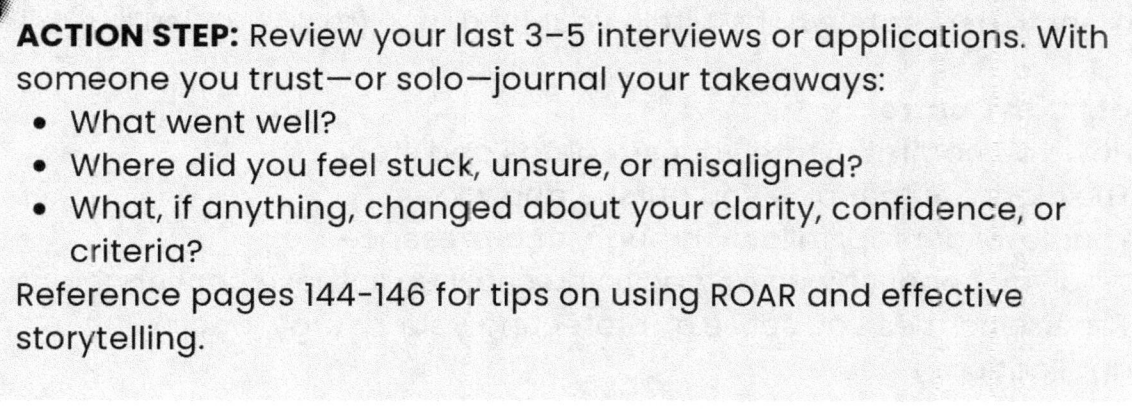

ACTION STEP: Review your last 3–5 interviews or applications. With someone you trust—or solo—journal your takeaways:
- What went well?
- Where did you feel stuck, unsure, or misaligned?
- What, if anything, changed about your clarity, confidence, or criteria?

Reference pages 144-146 for tips on using ROAR and effective storytelling.

What to Do When You Don't Hear Back

Not every "no" comes wrapped in an email. Sometimes, it's silence. Here's how to move forward:

- **Set Your Own Closure Point:** If you haven't heard back in 10–14 business days after a final interview, it's okay to assume the process has moved on. You can follow up once, but don't stay stuck waiting.
- **Don't Chase Closure—Create Clarity:** Use the lack of response as a chance to assess what you need going forward. Would you reapply to that company in the future? What did this process teach you about what you want (or don't)?
- **Document Learnings, Not Just Emotions:** Capture insights, tweaks to your approach, or new questions to ask in your next interview. Rejection becomes refinement when paired with reflection.
- **Keep Your Pipeline Warm:** Always have a few active leads in progress. That way, no single "no" holds too much power.

✒️ Reflection Prompt: What You Can Control vs. What You Can't

Not every outcome in the job search reflects your value or your effort. Take a moment to separate what's within your influence from what isn't.

What I Can Control:
- How you communicate your strengths and story
- The clarity of the roles you pursue and why
- Your level of prep, follow-through, and presence
- Who you connect with and how you show up in those conversations
- The boundaries you set (e.g., protecting your energy, pacing applications)
- Your mindset and willingness to keep going imperfectly

What I Can't Control:
- A hiring manager's unconscious biases or snap judgments
- Internal candidates already in play
- Budget freezes, reorgs, or paused roles mid-process
- Decisions based on one short conversation or group consensus
- Recruiters ghosting—not always malicious, sometimes just overwhelmed
- Personal dynamics you're not privy to (e.g., team tension, leadership changes)

Now, Reclaim Your Power:
- What's one thing I've been blaming myself for that might be out of my hands?
- What's one small action I can take this week that is fully within my control?

JOB SEEKER SPOTLIGHT

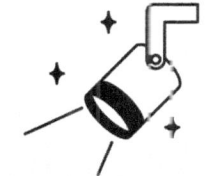

Turning Rejection Into Redirection

After being laid off from an Atlanta-based corporate retail role, **Sam** went through over a dozen interviews in just a few months—15, to be exact. Some processes stretched over multiple rounds. A few seemed promising. But none turned into offers.

The process was draining. At one point, Sam started to wonder—was he showcasing his impact, or just describing tasks? Instead of pushing through blindly, he paused. Reviewing past interviews, Sam spotted a pattern: he focused heavily on what he did, but rarely shared how he made decisions, solved problems, or approached challenges. His stories lacked the context and nuance that show employers how someone works, not just what they've done.

With this insight, Sam began reframing his examples using real job descriptions as practice prompts. He highlighted how he handled ambiguity, collaborated under pressure, and added value beyond what was asked. He practiced out loud with a friend until his delivery felt grounded and confident. Within weeks, the energy shifted. Sam landed a role that not only matched his skills but also his values and preferred work style, too.

Takeaway: Rejection is not always a red flag. It's feedback in disguise. When you pause, reflect, and adjust, the "no's" can point you toward a better aligned yes.

🏁 Momentum Builder: What I'm Learning From the Process

Use this tracker to capture insights, patterns, and growth from each opportunity, not just the outcome. Every step forward brings clarity and refinement.

Date	Role/ Company	Stage Reached	What Went Well	What I'd Refine Next Time	Any Feedback Received?	What Insights I Gained

Tips for Using This Tracker:

- Don't just fixate on missteps. Use 'What Went Well' to highlight repeatable strengths.
- Even without formal feedback, reflect on how the interaction felt, what surprised you, or what you'd do differently.
- Insights can be internal (what matters to you) or external (how different teams hire, communicate, or collaborate).

✍ Reflection Prompt:

Reflect on your last few applications or interviews. Are you consistently reaching a certain stage before being rejected? Write down what's working, what's not, and one strategy shift to test in your next application or interview.

Managing the Emotional Toll & Staying Motivated

☑ **Interrupt the Overthinking Loop:** It's natural to reflect, but constant replaying of interviews or applications can drain your energy. Capture lessons, then redirect your focus to the next step forward.

☑ **Acknowledge the Progress:** Every informational chat, interview, or skill practiced is movement. Celebrate the effort, not just the outcomes.

☑ **Prioritize Recovery:** Job searching is mentally and emotionally taxing. Build in intentional pauses like a day offline, a creative outlet, or time with someone who helps you feel like yourself. Rest is strategy.

ACTION STEP: Schedule a break this week to reset. Whether it's a full day offline, a creative hobby, or a no-job-talk coffee with a friend, recovery is part of strategy.

Expanding Your Strategy & Staying Proactive

☑ **Widen the Lens:** If rejections are piling up, it might be time to broaden your target. Consider adjacent industries, roles, or mission-driven sectors where your strengths transfer easily.

☑ **Deepen Relationships, Not Just Outreach:** The majority of roles are filled through referrals. Focus on genuine connection-building, not just requests, and keep your network warm, not just transactional.

☑ **Upskill with Purpose:** Even short, targeted learning (projects, certifications, AI tools, short courses) can boost both your confidence and marketability. Prioritize skills that are in demand in your target roles.

JOB SEEKER SPOTLIGHT

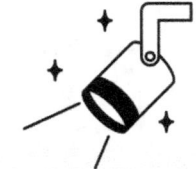

Rediscovering Fulfillment Through An Unexpected Pivot

After years supporting student success in learning assistance at a Florida university, **Jill** was laid off due to budget cuts. While disappointed, she initially saw it as a sign to pursue similar roles across the Southeast. With a strong resume, she secured several campus interviews, but after multiple rounds and six rejections, something wasn't landing.

Frustrated, Jill met with a career coach. In that honest conversation, she acknowledged what she'd been avoiding: her passion for learning assistance had quietly faded. Her answers in interviews, especially about future goals or recent professional development, lacked energy, and hiring teams could sense it.

It was time to realign. With a background in writing and editing, Jill decided to take a calculated risk and apply for a managing editor role, even though she met just 60% of the qualifications. To her surprise, she quickly connected with the editor-in-chief during the interview. Her authenticity and transferable skills stood out, and she received an offer shortly after.

Takeaway: Career paths evolve, and so do you. Sometimes clarity comes not from doubling down, but from asking what feels energizing now. Alignment often beats experience when it comes to making your next move.

✎ **Reflection Prompt:**

What part of your current career identity no longer fits—and what might you try instead?

PRO TIP: Today's job search is less of a straight path and more of a winding journey. Extended timelines, ghosting, and shifting priorities are increasingly common and rarely personal. Instead of tying your worth to unpredictable outcomes, track what you can influence: how you prepare, how you show up, and how you adapt. Progress isn't always linear, but intention always moves you forward.

Final Thoughts

Every "no" is a chance to sharpen your strategy, clarify what energizes you, and get closer to work that truly fits. Let each experience inform your path, not derail it. You're not starting from scratch; you're building from strength, with more clarity than you had before.

PHASE 3
Long-Term Career Security & Growth

Future-proof
Your Career

The world of work is changing faster than ever. Technologies like AI, automation, and real-time data tools are reshaping roles across industries, not just in tech. To stay relevant and resilient, today's professionals need more than experience. They need adaptability, curiosity, and a proactive approach to growth.

This chapter offers a practical, no-fluff framework to help you stay ahead of disruption, expand your opportunities, and build a career that evolves with the times.

Maximize Growth & Adaptability
Career advancement is no longer limited to titles or vertical moves. The most future-ready professionals invest in continuous learning, experiment with new pathways, and take ownership of their development.

✅ **Develop a Continuous Learning Mindset:** See skill-building as an essential part of your work, not something extra. Stay open to feedback, try new approaches, and treat challenges as growth labs.

✅ **Use Accessible Learning Platforms:** Explore free or low-cost learning options like:
- Google Career Certificates (e.g., UX Design, Project Management).
- Coursera & edX for university-backed courses in tech, leadership, and industry-specific trends.
- YouTube & LinkedIn Learning for quick skill refreshers.

✅ **Upskill from Where You Are:** Growth doesn't always require a new job. Stretch your skills by:
- Volunteering for cross-functional projects.
- Leading internal initiatives.
- Shadowing peers in other departments.
- Proposing a pilot project tied to an emerging trend in your industry

✅ **Experiment Without a Big Leap:** Test new interests with low-risk career experiments like:
- Freelance gigs
- Project-based consulting
- Hackathons or innovation challenges
- Volunteering in an adjacent field

Conduct a Future-Ready Skills Assessment

To stay competitive, you need to know what you already do well, and what the future demands next. Conducting a clear skills assessment helps you focus your time and energy where it matters most.

☑ **Step 1: Assess Your Current Skills.** Create a two-column inventory:
- *Column 1:* Current Skills (e.g., Excel, stakeholder engagement, cross-functional leadership)
- *Column 2:* Target Skills (based on job descriptions or industry trends)

☑ **Step 2: Identify the Gaps.** Use tools like:
- O*NET: Skill lists by job role.
- LinkedIn Skills Insights: Compare against top trending skills.
- Indeed or Coursera Skills Reports: Spot in-demand keywords and knowledge gaps.

☑ **Step 3: Build a Strategic Skills Plan.** Rather than learning everything, focus on high-value skills that:
- Align with your goals.
- Appear frequently in job descriptions.
- Have long-term relevance (e.g., AI literacy, systems thinking, data interpretation).

ACTION STEP: Choose one skill from your "Target Skills" column. Outline how you'll build it in the next 30 days through a course, real-world application, or mentorship conversation.

Expand Your Network & Opportunities

Career growth thrives through relationships, peer learning, and community. The more you diversify your professional connections, the more opportunities you create for future success.

☑️ **Engage in Peer-Led Development:** Join industry groups, online forums, and professional associations.

☑️ **Seek Out Mentors & Sponsors:** Connect with professionals inside and outside your field for guidance and perspective.

☑️ **Diversify Career Development Channels:** Consider learning from contractors, vendors, and clients, not just colleagues.

ACTION STEP: Reach out to one professional contact you admire and schedule a conversation to exchange career insights.

Stay Competitive & Future-Ready

Future-proofing is not about mastering every new trend. It's about anticipating change and evolving with purpose. Stay informed, intentional, and ready to pivot.

☑️ **Monitor Market & Tech Trends:** Follow labor reports, industry newsletters, and macroeconomic updates. Tools like the Bureau of Labor Statistics, Gartner, and Future of Jobs Report (WEF) offer strategic insight.

 Skills Forecasting and Industry Trends

"Act as a career strategist and labor market expert. Based on my background in **[insert role or industry]** and my goal to transition into **[target role or industry]**, what are the top 3–5 high-value or emerging skills I should prioritize to stay competitive over the next 2–3 years? For each skill, explain why it matters and recommend one relevant course, certification, or learning method I can explore."

☑️ **Leverage AI for Career Insights.** Use tools like:
- LinkedIn Career Explorer: to identify adjacent roles and upskill paths.
- O*NET & Eightfold.ai: to reveal hidden strengths and in-demand skills.
- Teal or Rezi: for job tracking and role-to-skill alignment.

☑️ **Prioritize Durable, Transferable Skills.** Invest in:
- Digital fluency (AI tools, data literacy)
- Human-centric leadership
- Adaptability & decision-making in complexity

 Tailored Skills Gap Analysis & Upskilling Strategy

"Act as a career strategist. I'm currently in **[insert current role or career stage]** and aiming to transition into **[insert target role]**. Based on this pivot, what are the top skill gaps I likely need to address? Create a comparison table of likely current vs. target skills, and recommend specific online courses, certifications, or self-directed projects to close each gap."

☑️ **Reframe Setbacks as Signals**

Restructuring? Shrinking budgets? Use disruption as an opportunity to solve high-impact problems and demonstrate your ability to lead through uncertainty.

ACTION STEP: Choose one of the following and commit to it this week:
☐ Based on everything you've explored in this chapter, choose one forward-looking action that feels both meaningful and manageable:
☐ Expand your skillset
☐ Strengthen a connection
☐ Rethink how your current strengths apply to what's next
Future-proofing is consistent steps toward staying relevant, resilient, and ready.

Final Thoughts

Career security is no longer about staying in the same role. It now depends on your ability to adapt, grow, and stay curious while making a meaningful impact. Whether you're evolving within your field or exploring new possibilities, proactive learning and meaningful connection are the throughlines to long-term success.

Explore Alternative Income Streams

A layoff often brings financial pressure, especially if the job search takes longer than expected. Alternative income streams offer flexible, short-term solutions that can help you stay afloat while keeping your skills sharp and uncovering new professional directions.

These options can serve multiple purposes: bridging the income gap, expanding your network, or even becoming the foundation for a long-term pivot. To help you weigh your options, here's a quick breakdown of common income streams—what they are, what they offer, and what to consider.

Types of Alternative Income Streams

Income Type	Definition	Key Considerations
Fractional Work	Part-time, high-level strategic roles (e.g., Fractional CMO, CFO)	Ideal for experienced professionals. Flexible but often requires juggling multiple clients
Contract Work	Fixed-term roles (e.g., 3–12 month contracts), often through staffing firms	Provides predictable income short-term; may lack benefits or long-term continuity
Temporary Work	Short-term assignments to cover leave or seasonal surges	Good for fast income. Often hourly with limited benefits and less strategic exposure
Gig Work	On-demand jobs like ride-sharing, delivery, or task-based services	Ultra-flexible but variable income and no benefits. Great bridge option for immediate cash flow
Freelance Work	Independent project-based work (e.g., writing, design, consulting)	Offers maximum independence. Requires marketing, contracts, and self-management

Where to Start: Real Platforms & Pathways

Now that you've reviewed the types of alternative income streams, here's how to take action, starting with platforms and ideas that align with your strengths, needs, and time.

Gig & Freelance Work: Flexible Income on Your Terms

For professionals looking to maintain autonomy or quickly generate income, gig and freelance options can offer immediate earning potential while building or reinforcing marketable skills.

☑ **Freelance Platforms:** Offer your services such as writing, design, programming, admin support, or consulting on platforms like:
- Upwork (broad range of projects)
- Fiverr (task-based gigs with tiered pricing)
- Toptal (premium talent network for seasoned experts)

☑ **Rideshare & Delivery Apps:** Flexible, fast-start income options:
- Uber, Lyft (rideshare)
- DoorDash, Instacart (food and grocery delivery)

Tip: Peak hours and batching orders increase your earnings potential.

☑ **Online Tutoring & Teaching:** Share your expertise remotely:
- VIPKid: Structured ESL for children (requires degree + TEFL/TESOL certification)
- Cambly: Casual conversation practice (no degree needed)
- Wyzant: Subject-based tutoring with control over rates and schedule

Contract, Fractional, & Temporary Work: Short-Term Roles, Long-Term Potential

These roles provide stability for a season and can lead to long-term opportunities, especially when used strategically.

☑ **Staffing & Talent Agencies**
- Partner with firms like Robert Half, Kelly Services, Adecco, or Creative Circle. Gain access to short-term roles that match your expertise.

☑ **Fractional Roles**
- Serve as a part-time expert in areas like marketing, operations, HR, or finance.
- Often ideal for experienced professionals looking to stay active across multiple organizations.

✅ Project-Based Consulting
- Companies may bring in contractors for specific deliverables (e.g., digital transformation, training design, process audits).
- Great for those who enjoy autonomy and focused work.

✅ Seasonal Jobs
- Industries like retail, hospitality, and logistics (e.g., UPS, FedEx) ramp up hiring during key times.
- Useful for fast income and entry into new fields.

PRO TIP: Don't try to explore every option at once. Choose one platform or pathway that feels aligned with your skills, schedule, and income goals and test it for 4-8 weeks. That's enough time to evaluate how it fits into your goals, without overcommitting or losing focus on your broader career plan. Track what energizes you, what pays off, and what's not worth repeating.

Beginner-Friendly Gig Ideas to Test

Not sure where to start? Here are three accessible options that allow you to earn while exploring your strengths. These are ideal for quick wins and skill-building, even if you've never freelanced before.

✅ Freelance Writing
- Start by publishing 1–2 sample articles on LinkedIn about a topic you know well. Use AI writing assistants to draft proposals for beginner gigs on platforms like Upwork or Contra.

✅ Virtual Assistance
- Offer basic admin support to small businesses—think inbox management, research, or scheduling. Use AI tools to generate your service descriptions and outreach emails.

✅ Online Tutoring or Teaching
- Record a short sample lesson and post it to LinkedIn or YouTube. Platforms like Cambly or Wyzant offer easy entry points. AI tools can help you write scripts or structure your teaching materials.

ACTION STEPS:
Choose one area above and take a low-stakes first step—create a LinkedIn post, set up a platform profile, or reach out to a contact who might need your help.

Part-Time & Remote Roles with Flexibiilty

These roles offer structured income and room to grow while still leaving time for job searching or upskilling:

- **Customer Support & Admin Assistance:** Many companies hire part-time remote help through platforms like Working Solutions and ModSquad.
- **Remote Sales & Marketing:** Look for contract roles in digital outreach, social media management, or affiliate marketing.
- **Retail & Logistics (Seasonal):** While not remote, major brands often have high-volume hiring cycles with quick onboarding.

Creative & Content-Based Income Paths

If you have a creative background or strong communication skills, these pathways let you monetize your talents in ways that are flexible, marketable, and scalable.

Visual & Audio Services

- Photography & Videography: Offer packages for events, product shoots, or brand storytelling. Market locally or on platforms like Thumbtack or Bark.
- Voiceover Work: Narration, commercials, and character work are in demand. Explore platforms like Voice123 and Voices.com.

Teaching & Coaching

- Creative Instruction: Offer lessons in music, writing, language, or design online (e.g., Lessonface, Superprof) or in-person.
- Skill-Based Coaching: Package your expertise into short-term coaching sessions (e.g., small business marketing, career storytelling, resume strategy).

Digital Content Services

- Content for Small Businesses: Provide social media management, video editing, email marketing, or copywriting services. Platforms like Contra, Fiverr, or freelancer networks are a good entry point.
- Creative Asset Development: Build templates, guides, or digital downloads that can be sold repeatedly on platforms like Gumroad or Etsy.

PRO TIP: If you're multi-skilled, choose one service to start and validate interest. Focus on delivering consistent value before expanding your offerings.

Testing a Business Idea While Job Searching

Starting a business doesn't have to be an all-or-nothing commitment. Use this time to validate an idea before fully transitioning.

☑️ **Launch Smart & Light**

- **Start with a Simple Offer (MVP):** Identify one clear, useful version of your service or product. Prioritize speed and value over perfection. Example: One-page guide, 30-minute coaching session, single workshop, or beta service.
- **Freelance to Test Demand:** Turn coaching, consulting, or digital skills into short-term projects. This builds both income and proof of concept.
- **Use No-Cost Business Tools:** Platforms like Canva (for branding), Teachable (for online courses), and Gumroad (for digital products) let you launch ideas quickly with little overhead.
- **Validate with Real Feedback:** Don't guess, ask. Run a small paid pilot, offer trials to trusted connections, or gather testimonials from early users Pre-orders and small commitments signal real interest.

 AI Prompt for Income Ideas

"Based on my background in **[your industry or skill set]**, what are 3–5 income-generating opportunities I could explore—such as freelancing, consulting, or teaching—that align with my strengths and current market demand? Please include niche ideas and suggested platforms to get started."
[insert strengths/skills]

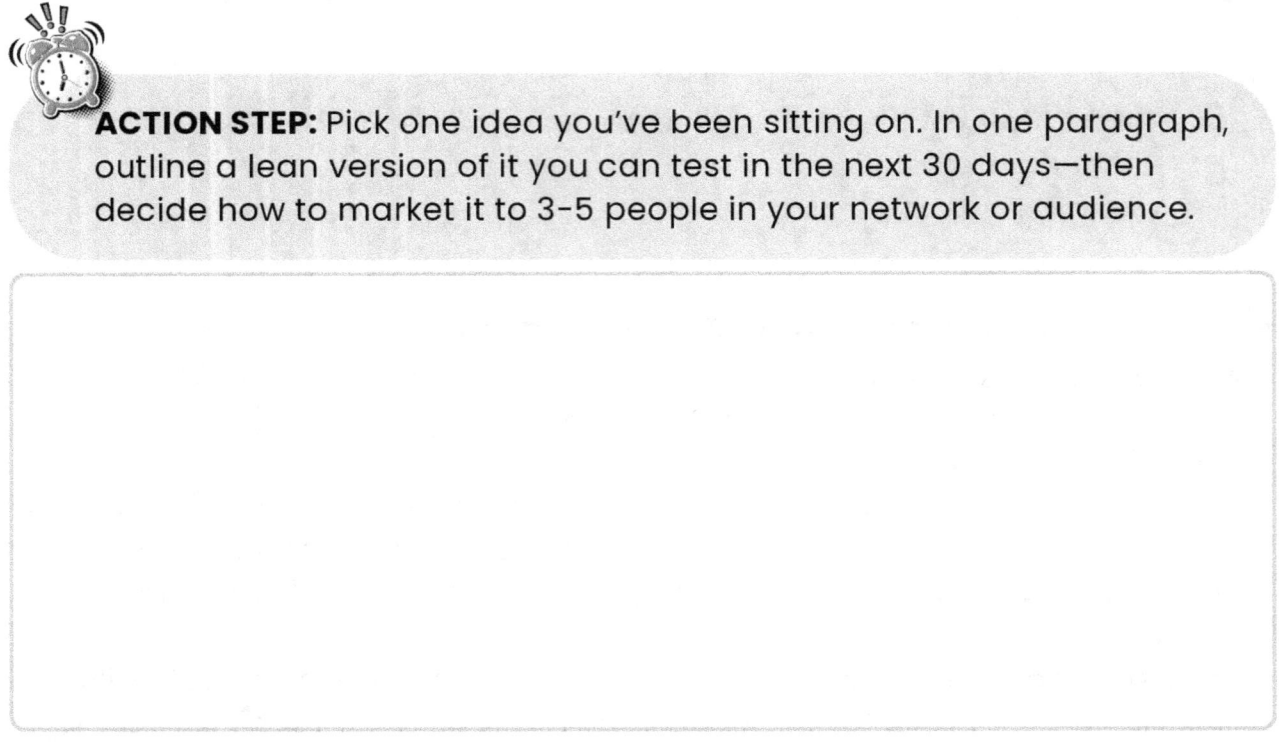

ACTION STEP: Pick one idea you've been sitting on. In one paragraph, outline a lean version of it you can test in the next 30 days—then decide how to market it to 3-5 people in your network or audience.

Transitioning Side Gigs into Full-Time Careers

When your side income begins to build traction, you may be closer to a full-time business than you think. Use that momentum intentionally.

☑ Grow with Intention

- **Scale Strategically:** Gradually raise rates, refine your offer, and grow your client base to match your capacity and value.
- **Build Predictable Income:** Diversify with recurring services, subscription models, or multiple income streams to reduce risk.
- **Balance Job Search and Business:** Use clear time blocks to stay productive without burning out, especially if you're still interviewing.
- **Set a Go/No-Go Milestone:** Choose an income or client benchmark that signals when it's time to go all in.

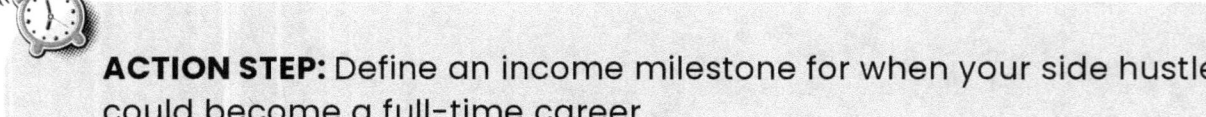

ACTION STEP: Define an income milestone for when your side hustle could become a full-time career.

Final Thoughts

Exploring alternative income streams is no longer a backup plan. It's a forward-looking career strategy. Whether you freelance, consult, teach, or test a business idea, these pathways let you stay financially afloat while building new skills, expanding your network, and uncovering what truly energizes you. Flexibility doesn't mean lack of direction, but staying open, agile, and in motion until the right opportunity or vision becomes clear.

Build Career Resilience Through Transition

Career resilience is about bouncing back *and* adapting forward. It's the ability to navigate uncertainty with clarity, respond to challenges with action, and maintain your well-being as you move toward what's next. Layoffs and transitions are tough, but they can also be turning points.

Reframe Your Mindset for Resilience

Resilience starts with what you believe about the situation and yourself.

☑ **Name What You're Feeling:** Layoffs often trigger grief-like responses (shock, frustration, sadness, acceptance). Acknowledge these emotions so they don't define your choices.

☑ **Rewrite the Narrative:** This transition is not a personal failure. It's a recalibration, a moment to pause, realign, and ask, *"What do I really want to build next?"*

☑ **Shift Into Action:** Instead of fixating on what happened, channel energy into what's next. Your job is not to control every outcome, but to own your response.

ACTION STEP: List 3 insights this transition has taught you about your strengths, adaptability, or values. These lessons are part of your resilience story and future interview narrative.

Sustain Resilience Through Supportive Habits

Once you've regained your footing post-layoff, sustaining progress requires intentional, restorative practices that support both your well-being and your goals.

✅ **Set Boundaries Around the Job Search:** Limit your time you spend applying or scrolling daily. Focus instead on high-impact efforts.

✅ **Lean Into Replenishing Routines:** Whether journaling, a creative outlet, or movement, anchor yourself in practices that restore clarity and focus.

✅ **Nurture Meaningful Connections:** Staying in touch with encouraging peers and mentors reinforces your motivation and sense of belonging.

✅ **Acknowledge Ongoing Progress:** Reflect on the internal shifts you've made, not just the external results.

✏️ **Reflection Prompt:**

What routines or connections have helped you stay grounded lately? How can you make space for more of them?

Activate Your Support Network Strategically

Your network is one of your most valuable assets during a career transition. Rather than viewing networking as a one-sided request for help, approach it as cultivating mutual, trust-based relationships that provide both opportunity and support.

Immediate Recovery Support Network

Start by reconnecting with people who can offer encouragement, insight, and quick-win leads.

☑️ **Reconnect with Peers Who Understand:** Reach out to former colleagues, especially those who've navigated similar transitions. Their experiences can provide emotional validation, referral potential, and practical advice.

☑️ **Tap Into Professional Resources:** If available, use outplacement services, resume reviews, and coaching support. These tools can help you reduce overwhelm and initiate moving forward

☑️ **Join Peer Support Spaces:** Explore digital communities and in-person groups that support job seekers. Options include:

- Local Job Clubs & Workforce Centers for resume help, interview practice, and local hiring intel.
- Alumni Career Centers offer mentorship, job boards, and networking directories.
- Layoff Alumni Networks where former employees share leads and insider knowledge.
- Online Forums (private Facebook groups or Slack channels) for accountability and shared experience.

Don't underestimate smaller or niche groups—these often offer faster, more personalized support than larger, general platforms.

☑️ **Balance Self-Care and Community Connection:** Maintain your energy by setting personal boundaries while actively engaging with networks that uplift your value and offer mutual encouragement.

☑️ **Embody Your Professional Identity:** Whether through affirming self-talk (e.g., *"I am capable and valuable during every season"*) or how you present yourself, online and offline, continue showing up as a professional with purpose, even during transition.

ACTION STEP: Create a "Community Wins Board" with your support circle, where you each record personal accomplishments, big or small. I maintain this in two ways: a dedicated group text with four fellow female entrepreneurs, and a waterfall of colorful Post-it notes displaying my goals and accomplishments in my workspace. This dual approach leverages positive social contagion through the group chat while providing immediate visual reinforcement when I need a private confidence boost. Try either approach—or both—depending on what resonates with you.

PRO TIP: To find support communities:
- Search "**[your city]** job club" or check your local library and community college websites
- Visit your college/university's career services website and alumni association page
- Check LinkedIn for "**[Company Name]** Alumni" or "**[Company Name]** Layoff Support" groups
- Explore industry-specific platforms like Blind, Fishbowl, or Reddit for invitation links

ACTION STEP: Join at least one new support group or professional forum this week. Look for a space where you can both learn and contribute. Introduce yourself, comment on a post, or initiate a conversation with another member to begin building supportive connections.

When Motivation Dips: What to Say to Stay Accountable

There will be moments in a transition when your energy drops, your momentum stalls, or you feel stuck in isolation. That's normal. Reaching out for encouragement, insight, or simply a sounding board can help you recalibrate and move forward with more clarity.

Here are a few low-pressure message scripts to help you reconnect with your network when you need support, but don't quite know how to ask:

☑ **If you're feeling stuck in your search:**

*"Hey **[Name]**, I've hit a bit of a wall in my job search and realized I could use some fresh perspective. Would you be open to a quick chat or even just sharing what's helped you stay grounded in times like these?"*

☑ **If you want accountability but don't want to burden others:**

*"Hi **[Name]**, I'm trying to stay more consistent with my job search goals and thought of you. Would you mind if I checked in from time to time for some light accountability and support? No pressure—just thought I'd ask."*

☑ **If you're reconnecting after time away:**

*"Hi **[Name]**, I've been in head-down mode navigating this career transition. I realized I miss talking with people who get it. Would you be open to reconnecting sometime soon?"*

PRO TIP: You don't need a perfect update or ask. Reaching out imperfectly is better than staying silent. People remember how you made them feel, not how polished your message was.

Final Thoughts

Resilience isn't built in a single moment but forged through the choices you make over time. From how you respond to setbacks to the support systems you engage and the skills you cultivate, every step shapes the foundation for what's next.

This season may feel uncertain, but it's also rich with possibility. When you stay connected to your values, take thoughtful action, and give yourself space to grow, reflect, reiterate, and rest, you build forward, stronger and more aligned than before. Let this transition be the start of something deeper: a career that reflects not just what you can do, but who you've become in the process.

Layoff Recovery Journal: Reflect, Reimagine, and Respond

Reflection is more than a release—it's a strategic tool. Journaling after a layoff helps you process emotions, reframe your story, and take purposeful action. This chapter offers practical prompts designed to support mindset shifts, renew your sense of identity, and rebuild forward momentum.
Use journaling as a self-coaching practice. It's your private space to unpack thoughts without judgment, reconnect with your values, and reclaim your voice, especially in moments that may have shaken your confidence.

Why Reflective Journaling Supports Career Recovery
Processes Emotional Weight: Lays down the burden of uncertainty, stress, and loss in a psychologically safe way.
Promotes Clarity & Self-Awareness: Helps uncover patterns, values, and strengths that might have gone quiet during survival mode.
Supports Strategic Planning: Translates reflection into direction—fueling aligned, confident career decisions.
Reinforces Resilience: Strengthens mental agility and emotional grounding, making setbacks easier to navigate.

Looking for a dedicated space to reflect? This playbook pairs well with **The Layoff Comeback Journal** for reflection and realignment.

 Scan the QR code to get your copy.

Structured Reflection Prompts

Use these prompts to shift your mindset from uncertainty to opportunity and document your progress.

Phase 1: Processing the Layoff

- How do I feel about this transition right now?
- What emotions am I experiencing now, and what might they be telling me?
- What parts of my previous job or identity am I ready to release?
- What did I genuinely enjoy—and want to carry forward?
- How can I see this layoff as a necessary interruption, not a permanent detour?

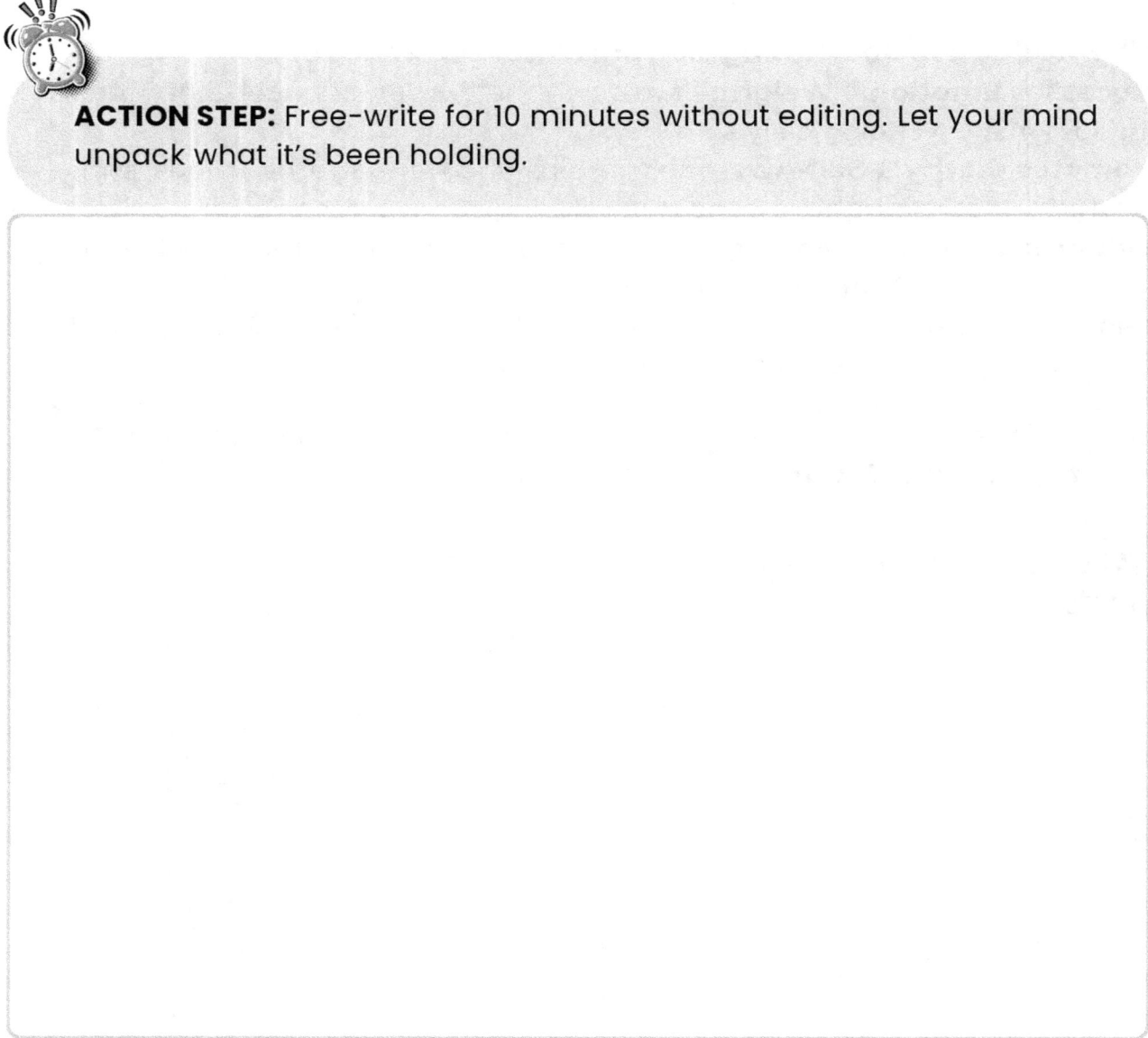

ACTION STEP: Free-write for 10 minutes without editing. Let your mind unpack what it's been holding.

Phase 2: Shifting Your Perspective

- What surprising lessons have emerged from this experience?
- What new possibilities has this transition revealed?
- What strengths have I demonstrated through past uncertainty or loss?

ACTION STEP: Write down one positive insight you've gained—and how it could shape your next step.

Phase 3: Rebuilding Confidence & Motivation

- What accomplishments, values, or skills affirm my value?
- When have I overcome adversity before, and what did it teach me?
- Who in my network energizes or encourages me right now?

Phase 4: Taking Strategic Action

- What's one low-pressure action I can take this week to regain momentum?
- What industries or roles am I curious to explore—and why?
- If I could design my next opportunity from scratch, what would it include?
- How will I continue building emotional and professional resilience long-term?

ACTION STEP: Choose any prompt from this section and write for 5–10 minutes. Then, jot down three personal strengths and one small action you can take today.

Before you close this chapter, consider how you'll make reflection part of your rhythm, not just a recovery tool but a habit that strengthens you for what's next.

Build a Ritual That Grounds You

Turning reflection into recovery requires rhythm. Creating a consistent close-out ritual after journaling gives your brain a cue that the work is done, for now, and allows the insights to settle. A grounding ritual doesn't need to be elaborate; it just needs to be repeatable and regenerative.

Here's how to create a journaling rhythm that supports your nervous system and your career growth:

✅ **Set a Time & Place:** Choose a consistent time to check in with yourself, whether it's morning reflection or evening wind-down. Find a quiet space or cozy corner that signals "this is my time."

✅ **Create a Sensory Anchor:** Pair your journaling with something grounding: a candle, playlist, warm drink, weighted blanket, or aromatherapy. These cues help train your brain to enter a reflective state more easily.

✅ **Use a Gentle Entry Point:** On hard days, use a low-pressure starter like:
- "Today I'm noticing..."
- "I feel most like myself when..."
- "Right now, I need..."

This lowers the barrier to entry and keeps the practice sustainable.

✅ **Track Wins, Not Just Worries:** Keep a running list of wins—big or small. This rewires your brain for progress, especially when self-doubt creeps in. Consider a visual system like Post-its, a "confidence jar," or a digital folder of encouraging messages and moments.

✅ **Share with Trusted Circles:** If it feels right, start a shared ritual with others like a "community wins board," text thread, or private voice note exchange with someone else navigating career change. Visibility multiplies motivation.

 **Final Thoughts**

Journaling is more than reflection. It's a quiet act of resilience. It helps you witness your own growth, gather insight from challenge, and find steady footing even in the face of uncertainty. You don't need all the answers to begin. You just need a place to be honest, intentional, and open to what's possible. This chapter, and season, is about rebuilding from the inside out. Keep showing up. Keep writing forward.

Afterword

If you made it this far, I hope you're starting to feel the shift.

From uncertainty to clarity.
From stuck to steady.
From "What now?" to "Watch me."

Career transitions are not just paperwork and profiles.
They're deeply human. Messy. Brave. Transformational.
And the truth is, this playbook is just the beginning.

Keep going.
Keep questioning.
Keep choosing yourself.

Because the next version of your career—and your life—isn't just possible.
It's already waiting for you to catch up.

With you every step.

Your Partner in Possibilities,

-Dr. Binta Brown

I'd Love Your Feedback!

Scan the QR code to tell me how this playbook supported your transition.

Your insights help improve this resource for others facing similar challenges.
- How did this playbook support your journey?
- What could make it even more helpful?

If this resource made a difference, consider leaving a 5-star review on Amazon so others can find support during their own transitions.

Thank you for being part of our community!

Remember: Career setbacks aren't the end of the story. They're an invitation to reflect, adapt, and move forward with purpose.

Notes

Notes

Notes

Notes

Notes

Notes

Notes

Notes